INNOVATION
PROWESS

T0025390

Available in the
Wharton Executive Essentials Series

Customer Centricity:
Focus on the Right Customers for Strategic Advantage
by Peter Fader

Financial Literacy for Managers:
Finance and Accounting for Better Decision-Making
by Richard A. Lambert

Global Brand Power:
Leveraging Branding for Long-Term Growth
by Barbara E. Kahn

Innovation Prowess:
Leadership Strategies for Accelerating Growth
by George S. Day

For more information,
visit *wsp.wharton.upenn.edu.*

WHARTON EXECUTIVE ESSENTIALS

GEORGE S. DAY

INNOVATION PROWESS

Leadership Strategies for
Accelerating Growth

WHARTON
SCHOOL
PRESS

Philadelphia

Published by Wharton School Press
The Wharton School
University of Pennsylvania
3620 Locust Walk
2000 Steinberg Hall-Dietrich Hall
Philadelphia, PA 19104

Email: whartonschoolpress@wharton.upenn.edu
Website: wsp.wharton.upenn.edu

Ebook ISBN: 978-1-61363-027-3
Paperback ISBN: 978-1-61363-028-0

9 8 7 6 5 4 3 2

Contents

Preface

Is your firm growing at its full potential?

Chances are the answer is no. And that's a problem.

The credible promise of superior growth from a stream of innovations is a powerful driver of a firm's stock price. Wall Street knows this, and so does management. This makes the pursuit of organic growth—growth both in the top line and in profit through internal means, rather than by acquisitions—a very high priority. For 26% of firms in 2010 it was their top priority. Another 71% said organic growth was one of their top three strategic priorities.[1] Yet most managers doubt they can reach the ambitious organic growth objectives sought by their firms.[2]

This book is for senior management teams charged with achieving the growth goals of their firms. It answers the strategic question of how you can accelerate your rate of organic growth in profits and revenues to one faster than your competitors. In other words, how do you unlock the full growth potential of your firm?

I have spent more than 25 years arriving at the answers to the organic growth challenge presented here. I have been pressed by demanding clients such as General Electric, W.L. Gore & Associates, Medtronic, TE Connectivity (formerly Tyco Electronics), Johnson & Johnson, and many others, and I have been inspired and provoked by participants in dozens of executive programs and strategy sessions, drawing support and insights from colleagues and other students of growth through innovation.

The answer I have come to about what growth leaders have that growth laggards don't can be summed up in the term *innovation prowess*. Innovation prowess has two facets: First, a highly disciplined growth-seeking process for setting ambitious but achievable growth objectives, with an outside-in approach to finding and selecting the best opportunities. Second, an equal commitment to investing in a *culture*, in *capabilities*, and in an organization *configuration* that support innovation and growth. Growth leaders marry these two facets in a virtuous, self-reinforcing cycle that allows them to convert their ambitions into profitable actions. This means they are able to commit sooner to better growth opportunities and bring them to market faster. Because the entire organization is aligned to growth, their success rates are much better than average. That's innovation prowess. My hope is that this book will enable readers to develop their own firms' innovation prowess.

I am drawn to the metaphor for writing a book that suggests it is like taking a caravan journey in ancient times. Success requires a clear view of the destination, guidance from other travelers on the same path, the resources and will to keep going, and the support of family, friends, and colleagues. I wish that I could single out all those who helped me start and continue the journey to completion of this book. Many have been a part of the Mack Center for Technological Innovation at the Wharton School of the University of Pennsylvania, whose mission is to advance the practice of innovation in organizations; notably, my colleagues Harbir Singh, Nicolaj Siggelkow, Karl Ulrich, and Paul Schoemaker and senior fellows Terry Fadem, Larry Huston, and Daniel Zweidler, from whom I have learned much. This innovative hub in a knowledge network has been generously supported by William and Phyllis Mack, for which I am very grateful. Special thanks go to my colleagues David Robertson and Saikat Chaudhuri for their thoughtful feedback on earlier versions of this book, and to Christine Moorman at Duke University's Fuqua School of Business, who was a great help during the development of my thinking.

This journey was started with an invitation from Steve Kobrin and Shannon Berning to consider a book for Wharton Digital Press (later renamed Wharton School Press) in the Wharton Executive Essentials Series. Their encouragement and editorial prowess have made this a better book. Tim Ogden of Sona Partners was a guide for this journey, by taking the reader's point of view to rewrite and shape the ideas into a persuasive narrative.

This book is dedicated to my children, Sharon, Geoffrey, and Mark, who give me inspiration, and to my wonderful, loving wife, Alice, whose enthusiasm for this project and unfailing support have sustained me.

George S. Day
Villanova, Pennsylvania
January 21, 2013

Introduction:
The Growth Challenge

Is your firm struggling to grow because of the following issues?

- It has trouble moving successfully from ideas to impact?
- It regularly fails to anticipate emerging opportunities and has to react to competitors?
- The productivity of its innovation activities is falling behind that of your rivals?
- Turf battles and short-term pressures routinely pull innova tion resources from ambitious long-term growth initiatives?
- The culture is inward looking and risk averse?
- No one is held accountable for missed growth projections?

If these are pressing issues, you're not alone.

For all the veneration of innovators in the business and popular press, few firms have a solid grasp of how to drive superior organic growth. But such firms do exist—and prosper. Growth leaders such as IBM, Nike, American Express, Lego, and Amazon consistently realize organic growth rates exceeding those of their rivals. The purpose of this book is to learn from these growth leaders.[3] With the strategies, processes, and methods discussed in this book you can build a tested and comprehensive template for accelerating your firm's organic growth rate.

Peter Drucker, one of the foremost thinkers in management practice, viewed innovation as a discipline, a skill that could be learned and practiced, like playing a musical instrument. He believed that innovation was about devising a systematic way of identifying opportunities that provide new value for customers and exploiting them with disciplined work: "What all successful entrepreneurs I have met have in common is not a certain kind of personality but a commitment to the systematic practice of innovation."[4]

But Drucker's vision is rarely seen in practice. More often companies are like ActivatorCo, a leading firm in hydraulic systems used to lift elevators and move airplane flaps, with which I consulted. ActivatorCo suffered from having too many projects to absorb with its limited resources. It was entering a number of new markets and expanding its product lines while shifting from hydraulic to linear induction technologies. Few projects were completed properly. Instead of fully prepared "product releases" with tested new products, the company had "product escapes." It felt pressured to push new products out the door without adequate sales training, documentation, or support, which spawned a host of problems that had to be fixed later. Its growth was faltering, the organization was demoralized, and leadership was frustrated.

Firms such as ActivatorCo are well intentioned but ineffectual. They want to grow, but their organization gets in the way. Instead of being growth leaders, they are growth laggards. For growth laggards, increasing investment in R&D or other parts of the innovation value chain often doesn't just fail to pay off; it make things worse. The problem isn't typically lack of funding, opportunities, or even ambition. It's lack of innovation prowess.

Growth Laggards vs. Leaders: The Difference Is Innovation Prowess

Innovation prowess is gained by combining strategic *discipline* in growth-seeking activities with an organizational *ability* to achieve the aspirations and intentions of the growth strategy. Both facets work together to accelerate organic growth to a rate faster than competitors—and then sustain that rate.

Growth leaders have a superior ability to innovate that gives them confidence to commit to a strategy of accelerated growth. Their disciplined approach to growth uses that ability to pick the best growth pathways to pursue, ensure they have the resources to succeed, and then execute well. Because the strategic front end is in place, and the whole organization is aligned to growth, the odds of market success of individual growth initiatives are much greater. Conversely, growth laggards have an anemic innovation ability, so they can't consider ambitious growth strategies, which further degrades their confidence in their ability.

Thomas Edison famously said, "Genius is one percent inspiration and ninety-nine percent perspiration." Growth leaders are surely inspired by their growth strategies, but they also sweat the execution and fulfillment of their strategy by applying their organization ability. Their ability provides them with organization muscle from three reinforcing elements:

1. An innovation *culture* that encourages risk taking and exploration;
2. The *capabilities* exercised through innovation processes for acquiring deep market insights, mastering the supporting technologies, and carrying out innovation activities better than their rivals; and
3. A *configuration* of the organization and incentives that support and encourage growth-seeking behavior.

These are the "three Cs" that, when married with disciplined growth-seeking and growth-realizing processes, yield innovation prowess.

The innovation prowess of growth leaders enhances their ability to move from ideas to impact in three ways: First, by motivating all parts of the organization to take attractive opportunities through to completion and recognizing and rewarding innovation advocates; second, by removing obstacles that limit their potential to grow; and third, by strengthening the ability to innovate by opening up the organization to outside resources, nurturing the best talent, and supporting continuous learning.

It takes sustained leadership and the long-run commitment of finance and human resources to build innovation prowess. Success begets success: Prowess improves the more it is applied.

But it can be degraded by management neglect, complacency, overconfidence, and, especially, the pressure for short-term results. Thus, Nokia lost ground in the burgeoning smartphone market by emphasizing short-run earnings to sustain its share price, a consequence of which was an unwillingness to invest to replace its aging Symbian platform. This underinvestment left Nokia unable to match the customer experience of the Apple iPhone or the versatility and openness of the Android platform. Many observers point to a lack of diversity in the company's leadership team—setting the stage for inward-looking "group think"—as one reason why Nokia was so slow to realize its predicament. Most of the leaders were lifetime Nokians who'd grown up with mobile phones but who had less experience or feel for fast-moving Internet-based markets.

Growth leaders in very diverse industries, with utterly different histories, use a similar mantra when it comes to innovation and growth: "Think big...Start small...Fail cheap...Scale fast." This approach helps overcome the centripetal pull of innovation resources toward cautious, low-yield initiatives in favor of bolder opportunities with higher risk-adjusted returns. These bolder ideas typically include innovations far beyond products or features and engage every function of the business. Growth leaders explicitly seek out growth opportunities that come from improving the customer experience, moving into adjacent product or geographic markets, and changing their business model. The growth opportunities that emerge from these innovations are often more profitable than any technical marvel on a sliver of silicone.

Growth leaders further enhance their innovation prowess by grounding every step of their growth-seeking process in deep market insights, with the aim of creating new value—not just new things—for customers. Growth leaders take an outside-in view that guides the search for innovation from the perspective of existing and potential customers and competitors. Sophie Vandebroek, CTO of Xerox, sums up this approach to innovation this way: "If you innovate and it doesn't end up as something the customer benefits from, then it's not innovation."[5]

A Disciplined Process Is the First Step Toward Accelerating Growth

How do growth laggards begin to develop innovation prowess and take steps toward becoming growth leaders? The first step is implementing a disciplined growth-seeking process.

Organizations use many kinds of innovation processes to realize their growth aspirations. These can be split into two categories: growth-seeking and growth-realizing. The growth-seeking process is all the steps taken to set a strategic direction, seek opportunities, and select the best from among them. The growth-realization process comprises all the steps taken to bring these opportunities to market and sell them. I'll leave the innards of the growth-realization process to others; in this book, I'll focus on the growth-seeking process.

At the top of the hierarchy of the subprocesses that make up the growth-seeking process is the setting of a growth strategy that guides the search for opportunities, sets growth objectives, details the resources needed, and mobilizes everyone with a role in innovation. The growth strategy provides a blueprint for operational activities, including stage-gate development processes for individual projects, brainstorming for ideas in a domain of interest, or identifying and selecting innovation partners.

The growth-strategy-setting process is the antidote to the old saying "If you don't know where you are going, any road will take you there." Knowing the road—or, more accurately, knowing the compass heading to follow—gives meaning and direction to the whole organization. Organic growth can then be sought in a systematic way. Without this discipline, the pursuit of growth will inevitably be haphazard and episodic. This is not a method for confidently addressing the future.

The aim of the growth-seeking process is to achieve high productivity in the application of innovation resources and ability, by seeing the best opportunities sooner than rivals and then reducing errors of commission (pursuing dry holes that absorb scarce resources) and omission (missing big opportunities). Every company has its "Why didn't we do that?" list: Why didn't:

- Sony provide online music (instead of Apple)?
- Local newspapers offer online classified ads (instead of Craigslist)?
- Nordstrom see sooner the possibility of selling shoes online (instead of Zappos)?
- Microsoft launch an Internet-based advertising medium (instead of Google)?
- Kodak sell a full line of digital cameras and photo printers (instead of Canon)?
- LEGO build an online construction game (as Mojang did with Minecraft)?

There is an emerging view among growth leaders and students of innovation about how best to embed the growth strategy into the overall business strategy, and the necessary stages of the process for seeking growth.[6] These stages are connected in the sequential learning process in the three steps at the top of Figure I-1. This growth-seeking process accepts the reality that innovation is inherently inefficient; that is the essence of its exploratory, trial-and-error, risk-taking nature. An effective growth-seeking process balances divergence (which widens the search for opportunities) with convergence, to focus on the best bets. This balance is easy to lose. As top-down pressure for organic growth intensifies, the number of growth initiatives usually expands faster than the capacity of the organization to bring them to market. The inevitable result is an internal traffic jam of projects that causes delays, frustrations, and disappointment. Jørgen Vig Knudstorp, CEO of the LEGO Group, rightly observes, "Companies don't die of starvation, they die of indigestion."

Figure I-1
Innovation Prowess: Discipline + Ability

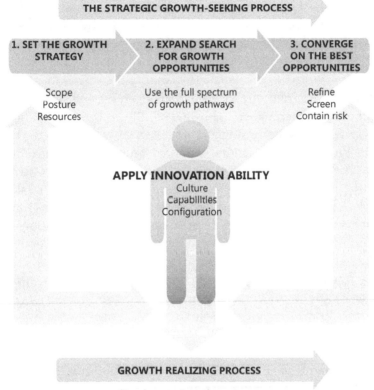

THE STRATEGIC GROWTH-SEEKING PROCESS

1. SET THE GROWTH STRATEGY	2. EXPAND SEARCH FOR GROWTH OPPORTUNITIES	3. CONVERGE ON THE BEST OPPORTUNITIES
Scope Posture Resources	Use the full spectrum of growth pathways	Refine Screen Contain risk

APPLY INNOVATION ABILITY
Culture
Capabilltles
Configuration

GROWTH REALIZING PROCESS

Develop ▸ Launch ▸ Learn

As noted in Figure I-1, a disciplined growth-seeking process includes setting a growth strategy, expanding the search for growth opportunities, and converging on the best opportunities. These steps are fed by (and feed on) the three Cs of culture, capabilities, and configuration, which determine innovation ability. When they come together, as illustrated in Figure I-1, the result is innovation prowess. Thus, Figure I-1 is the framework for this book. Of course, there is another set of steps to profiting from innovation—the growth-realizing process at the bottom of Figure I-1—that, as noted earlier, is *not* the focus of this book. I'll leave the development and launch activities for bringing innovation to market in the hands of the many experts who have discussed them at the individual project level.

Each of the following chapters deals with a specific stage of the growth process, and the development of innovation prowess. Chapter 1 focuses on setting a growth strategy that is realistic and achievable while still pushing the firm to raise its growth rate. Chapter 2 turns to the issue of expanding the search for growth opportunities. I've developed a road map for this search that follows what I term the 14 pathways of full-spectrum innovation.[7] Chapter 3 takes on the difficult process of converging on the best bets; choosing and pursuing a limited number of opportunities that the firm can hope to bring to market successfully, with the right balance of risk and reward. Finally, in Chapter 4, I'll take a look at the people side of the equation, by showing how growth leaders nurture and exercise their innovation prowess through an artful integration of their culture, capabilities, and configuration. Innovation prowess requires a disciplined growth process, but it is not all about processes. Processes don't have insights, find creative solutions to problems, or connect with customers. Only people do that. If your growth strategy isn't supported by, and supportive of, an organization with the culture, capabilities, and configuration necessary to nurture organic growth, your efforts to develop and apply innovation prowess will surely disappoint.

Building superior innovation prowess cannot be done easily or quickly. Many firms will aspire to become growth leaders but will fall short, either because of a lack of knowledge or a shortage of determination. This book can help management teams accelerate their growth rate with a tested and comprehensive approach to building their innovation prowess. By giving them a clear path forward, this guide to action can also strengthen their determination to make the necessary investments. There has never been a better time to make this commitment, as customers are more demanding and the competitive landscape more challenging, and as technological advances are opening up more exciting new ways to deliver value to customers.

Chapter 1

Set the Growth Strategy

A growth strategy is a statement of growth ambition and direction. It is less like a road map—which has a definitive path and set landmarks—than a compass setting. The purpose of a growth strategy is to give direction to the search for opportunities, establish resource requirements, guide significant strategic choices, and mobilize the entire organization. Because it is clear about the destination, it allows you to judge each choice in terms of its usefulness in reaching that destination.

As I explain in this chapter, a useful growth strategy addresses four issues:

1. *Growth objectives:* How fast do we want to grow revenues and profits? What must be invested now to realize future targets and close the growth gap?
2. *Scope and boundaries:* How broadly should the business search for growth opportunities? What choices are out of bounds?
3. *Strategic posture:* Will the business be a first mover, a fast follower, or a niche explorer in mature markets? Will the business have an open or closed approach to innovation? What is the desired balance between growth through acquisition and organic growth?
4. *Allocation of resources:* What proportion of the people and financial resources should be allocated to protecting the core business, versus investing in initiatives that are riskier and longer term?

Praxair demonstrates the rewards that can come from a clearly articulated growth strategy.[8] In 2004 this global maker of industrial gases set out to find \$2 billion in revenue growth over five years. One half was to come from acquisitions; the other half required double-digit organic growth at the rate of \$200 million per year. This was far beyond the annual growth that could be realized from repackaging helium, hydrogen, oxygen, and other gasses, the firm's core business. The organic growth goal was broken down into actionable categories: The first 15% would come from incremental growth in the base business and new channels for serving current markets; the rest would come from new services, such as nitrogen injection of oil and gas wells, servicing the helium coolant used in MRI magnets, and developing new reactor cooling and nitrogen injection cooling methods for the bioscience industry. These growth initiatives came from an intimate knowledge of the changing customer needs that could be met with Praxair's existing capabilities in industrial gas production and delivery and its mastery of combustion, freezing, and metal-fabrication technologies.

Praxair's growth strategy allowed management to set goals, allocate resources, recognize investment needs, and evaluate progress. The lead role in exploring the market, articulating and screening the opportunities, and orchestrating the specific projects was assigned to marketing, with sustained top management support and oversight. As a result of these decisions, revenues increased from $6.59 billion in 2005 (with net income of $697.0 million) to $10.12 billion in 2010 (with net income of $1.20 billion)—despite a collapse in some of the company's key markets such as steel and autos in the 2008–2009 recession.

Designing your growth strategy requires systematically working through the elements. First you must set realistic growth objectives. This is a two-step activity: calibrating the growth gap, and then assessing the potential of the existing portfolio of growth initiatives to close the gap. Invariably there will be a shortfall. With the growth gap in mind, you specify the scope and boundaries of the search for additional growth opportunities. Next, you have to articulate your strategic posture in regard to how growth opportunities will be discovered and developed. The final step is to ensure that adequate resources are allocated to realize the growth objectives.

Setting the Growth Objectives: Can We Close the Growth Gap?

Objectives for future growth in revenue and operating profits emerge from an iterative and often emotional dialogue. The negotiations begin with the management team setting growth targets that will achieve stakeholder goals. This often requires pushing the business to the limit of its capabilities. Shareholders' insistence on getting a superior rate of return on their investment requires growing faster than competitors and taking better advantage of investment opportunities.

Since growth objectives are usually set from the top down, there is often a wide gap between increasingly aggressive targets and increasingly risk-averse portfolios of growth initiatives. In my work studying or consulting with dozens of companies, I have consistently seen that the top-down growth objectives usually do not reflect the momentum of the business or the prospects, timing, or riskiness of the firms' existing growth initiatives. There is a strong temptation for senior managers to set growth goals higher than is realistic in order to satisfy shareholders. This is especially true if senior management is divorced from customer, market, and innovation feedback.

Designing a workable growth strategy begins with a realistic look at growth trends and momentum versus the growth objectives. The pivotal question is whether the available growth initiatives can close the growth gap between objectives and the momentum. To understand what is achievable, rather than what is desired, management first needs to dissect the sources of past growth and make realistic forecasts for each source of future growth.[9]

Assessing the Growth Gap

The starting point is the decomposition of revenue growth from prior years. When looking at the last three to five years, giving more weight to the recent past is ideal. This exercise is about establishing a realistic view of the sources for potential revenue growth.

Growth analysis requires categorizing prior growth in order to understand sources and trends. Often management teams are caught in an inside-out frame when analyzing growth. Such a frame focuses on accounting categories and product lines rather than on customers. This is a mistake. A better approach is to analyze growth in terms of six customer-centered categories, sorted by the range of strategies that are possible. Figure 1-1 gives an example. Four of these six sources of growth are derived from the core business:

- Sales from served market expansion, assuming market share stays constant (growth of market)
- Gains from price changes
- Reducing losses from churn
- Gross market share changes

Cutting losses from churn or customer defections can be an important source of growth—the average firm has a churn rate of 18% per year. Cutting this churn by, say, 2% means an increase of 2% in the top line.

The other two sources of growth are expansions from the core business. These include expansion into adjacent markets or geographies and bolder initiatives to expand into brand-new product areas, geographies, or business models.

Figure 1-1
Analyze the Sources of Organic Growth*

*Excludes the effects of acquisitions

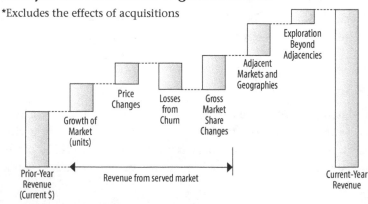

Calibrating the Growth Gap

The next step is momentum forecasting. The goal is to assess where sales and profits will be in two, three, or five years if the present strategy and trends continue without major changes. This may sound simple. It's not. The management team has to agree on their beliefs and assumptions about the future of the business. Momentum is not the same as inertia, because it presumes appropriate adaptations to market forces and a continuing quest for improvement. The momentum will be shaped by all the forces that will inhibit or facilitate growth in revenue and profits, including market growth, competitive pressures on share and margins, and potential productivity gains. Don't forget to include the contribution of growth initiatives ready to be launched.

All momentum forecasting is speculative; the farther out you forecast, the higher the uncertainty. One way to address this is to forecast best-case and worst-case scenarios and create a "cone of uncertainty" (see Figure 1-2). The farther into the future one looks, the greater the cone of uncertainty around the key assumptions and the greater the spread between the best-case and worst-case scenarios.

Closing the Growth Gap

The next step is to compare the growth trends and momentum with the existing growth objectives. Typically this will show a significant gap between the firm's momentum and the growth objectives, as shown in Figure 1-2.

Why do so many firms find it hard to close their growth gap? One school of thought emphasizes external constraints: Companies are mired in saturated "Red Ocean" markets, pressured by customers who themselves are squeezed, and forced to compete for incremental share gains with rivals who follow similar strategies.[10] Other pathologists of the problem point to internal impediments: short-term incentives that subvert long-term objectives; urgent demands from customers and salespeople that absorb scarce development resources; and a general lack of innovation prowess.[11]

Figure 1-2
Momentum Forecasting and the Growth Gap

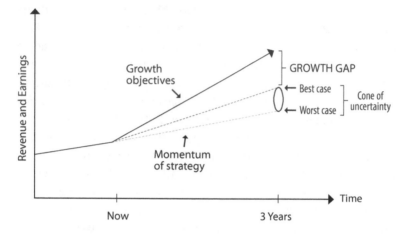

The combined effect of these external and internal impediments is that "small-*i*" innovation displaces "BIG-*I*" (major) innovation. Most growth initiative portfolios are heavily tilted toward the small-*i* end of the continuum of degrees of innovation:

Small-*i* ⟷	BIG-*I*
• Exploitation of existing capabilities	• Exploration of new market spaces
• Incremental	• Breakthrough
• Continuous improvement	• Disruptive/discontinuous change
• Red Ocean (from the blood of competitors)	• Blue Ocean (uncontested white space)
↓	↓
Low risk—small rewards	High risk—large rewards

Small-*i* innovations make up 85 to 90% of most companies' innovation portfolios but rarely generate much additional growth. The result is internal traffic jams of safe, incremental initiatives that delay all projects, stress organizations, and fail to achieve revenue or earnings goals. What's more, small-*i* projects tend to drain R&D budgets as companies struggle to keep up with customers' and salespeople's demands for a continuous flow of incrementally improved products. Meanwhile, there is an aversion to BIG-*I* initiatives, which stems from a belief that they are too risky and their rewards (if any) will accrue too far in the future.

Assessing Risk

To assess its innovation portfolio, a firm needs a clear picture of where its various growth initiatives fall on the spectrum of risk and reward, from small-*i* to BIG-*I*. The "innovation risk matrix" employs a unique scoring system and calibration of risk to help estimate the probability of success or failure for each initiative based on how big a stretch it is for the firm.[12]

Each growth initiative is plotted on two dimensions: how familiar the firm is with the intended market, and the similarity of the product/technology to existing offerings. This matrix has many sources, including long-buried consulting reports and post-audits of product and service innovations I conducted years ago while advising a consortium of firms studying innovation and growth challenges. Failure is defined as missing by more than 35% the original financial and market objectives used to justify the project. The results are consistent with recent surveys that place the overall failure rate of new products close to 40%. The ranges in probabilities within the "rainbow bands" are due mainly to differences in the ability of firms to manage risk and avoid unnecessary failures.

Most firms find that when they plot all their growth initiatives on this matrix, the majority clusters in the low-risk/ low-return corner on the lower left. Relatively few projects are either moves into an adjacent market or BIG-*I* initiatives which promise substantial organic growth at higher risk. This imbalance is unhealthy, if unsurprising. Discounted-cash-flow analysis and other financial yardsticks for evaluating development projects are usually biased against the delayed payoffs and uncertainty inherent in BIG-*I* innovations.

Figure 1-3
The Innovation Risk Matrix

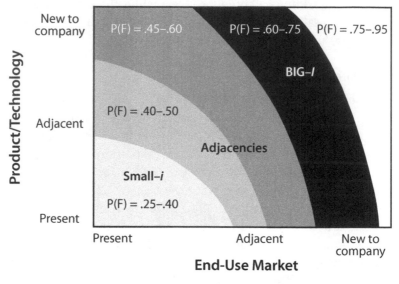

P(F)=Probability of Failure

Growth Potential of the Innovation Portfolio

The next step in setting realistic growth objectives is to diagnose the existing innovation portfolio, including new products and plans to enter new markets. There are many ways to display the portfolio of all growth initiatives the business is actively pursuing. I use the innovation risk matrix because it provides a clear picture of how the projects fall on the spectrum of risk, and the potential of the portfolio. It may be surprisingly difficult to compile all the growth initiatives that are under way. R&D will know all about technology and new product initiatives. But other growth initiatives may be dispersed through the organization: Marketing may be exploring a new end-use market with a joint venture partner, while senior management may be investing in early-stage start-ups, or considering a business model innovation.

Next, position each growth initiative in the innovation risk matrix. An initiative's position will be determined by its score on a range of factors, such as how closely the behavior of targeted customers will match that of the company's current customers, how relevant the company's brand is to the intended market, and how applicable the company's technology capabilities are to the new product. A template for positioning the growth initiative can be found in Appendix A.

Positioning a particular project on the matrix requires deep insight. When McDonald's attempted to offer pizza, for example, it assumed that the new offering was closely adjacent to its existing fast-food items, and thus targeted its usual customer. Under that assumption, pizza would be a familiar product for the present market and would appear in the bottom left of the innovation risk matrix. But the project failed, and a postmortem showed that the launch had been fraught with risk. No one could figure out how to make or serve a pizza in 30 seconds or less, and orders caused long backups at the takeout window, violating the McDonald's service-delivery model.

I recommend that an analysis of the existing growth portfolio be undertaken by a portfolio review team typically consisting of senior managers with strategic oversight and authority over development budgets and allocations. Team members rate each project independently and then explain their rationale. They discuss reasons for any differences of opinion and seek consensus. The overall health of the portfolio is revealed by the plot of all initiatives (with each initiative represented by a dot whose size is proportional to the project's estimated revenue). The portfolio in Figure 1-4, dominated by relatively low-risk, low-reward projects, is typical of most firms' innovation portfolios.

The final step is to forecast the risk-adjusted revenues and profits likely to be realized from each of the initiatives in the innovation portfolio. Their contribution to closing the growth gap depends on (a) how likely they are to be developed, (b) when they are likely to be launched, and (c) their probability of success when they enter the market. These individual contributions are then cumulated across the portfolio for each year of the planning horizon. The larger the growth gap, the less the innovation portfolio is likely to close it in the foreseeable future.

Figure 1-4
The Innovation Portfolio*

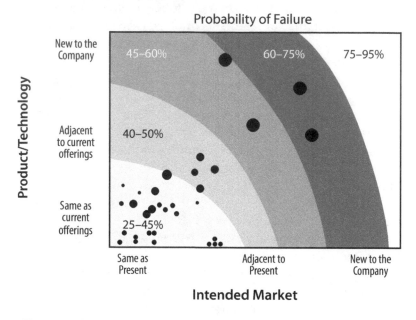

*The areas of the circles reflect the expected size of the sales (and/or profits) of the project relative to the other projects in the portfolio.

Once the growth gap is reassessed in light of the available growth initiatives, you'll likely need to begin negotiating trade-offs in the objectives. It may be possible to achieve the revenue growth objective but not the earnings objective—or vice versa. Still, there is almost always a widening growth gap to be filled with a search for better opportunities. But where should the search be directed?

Establishing Scope and Boundaries

When confronting the reality of a large growth gap and an innovation portfolio bereft of BIG-*I* or attractive adjacency projects, some managers and executives may panic. In this case, panic takes the form of an undisciplined search for big ideas and a willingness to accept ideas that are too risky or simply beyond the reach of the firm. While ambitious growth objectives require stretching for opportunities beyond the currently served markets and business models, savvy managers and executives know they need to put limits on how far they reach.

The Value of Limits

The legendary LEGO Group offers a cautionary tale in the pitfalls of stretching the scope too far. In the late 1990s the company followed the advice to "think outside the box," and launched forays into video games, movies, theme parks, and learning centers, in search of new play experiences.[13] The majority of these initiatives lost money, and pushed the LEGO Group near to bankruptcy by 2003. In response, management refocused the company's innovative activities on the traditional play experience it was known for, and sharply limited how much was devoted to creating new experiences. Less was more, and LEGO has regained its mojo as one of the premier innovators.

A disciplined approach to setting boundaries and limits should aim to help the organization answer the following questions:

- Which areas are desirable because they support the core business? (These are the small-i initiatives necessary to maintain competitiveness.)
- Where to seek new growth opportunities that stretch but don't strain the innovation ability, so managers can understand their degrees of freedom?
- What is unthinkable because it would divert resources with little chance of being pursued?

Growth leaders approach these questions in two ways. First, they start their thinking process from the outside in, and look at their growth prospects by standing in the shoes of their customers, channel partners, and competitors. Second, they seek adjacencies, because these promise the best balance between risk and reward by drawing on the existing knowledge and capabilities of the business.

Xerox has successfully moved beyond its traditional boundaries with an adroit combination of acquisitions and organic initiatives into adjacencies. The first step came in 2009 with its purchase of Affiliated Computer Services, which had built a 74,000-employee document-management firm serving corporations, state governments, and law—often using non-Xerox equipment. This was the launching pad for an expanded scope beyond copiers, printers, and document handling, to help companies transform very complex and burdensome business processes. To support this drive into services, Xerox developed Web-based document tools to help banks streamline the mortgage approval process and law firms search and manage millions of documents.

Start from the Outside In

With an outside-in mind-set, the growth strategy dialogue starts with the market. The top team steps outside the boundaries of the company as it is and looks first at its market: How and why are our customers changing? What new needs do they have? How can we help them solve their problems and become more successful? How can we meet the needs of nonconsumers; what are the barriers that inhibit consumption? What new competitors are lurking around the corner, and how can we derail their efforts?

Jeff Bezos, the cofounder and chairman of Amazon.com, is an advocate of this approach. He explained how Amazon was able to meet customers' need for Web services (by offering access to its cloud computing network) and for a more convenient reading experience (with the Kindle). He describes it as a "working backward" mentality:

> Rather than ask what we are good at and what else can we do with that skill, you ask, who are our customers? What do they need? And then you say we're going to give that to them regardless of whether we have the skills to do so, and we will learn these skills no matter how long it takes....There is a tendency I think for executives to think that the right

course of action is to stick to the knitting—stick with what you are good at. That may be a generally good rule, but the problem is the world changes out from under you if you are not constantly adding to your skill set.[14]

Inside-Out Thinking

Inside-out thinking asks what core assets and capabilities the firm already has that can be mobilized and leveraged. An example of building on existing capabilities is Corning Glass. During the dot.com bubble, Corning Glass soared by riding the booming demand for the fiber-optic cable in communication networks. After the crash, and a plunge in the share price from $100 to $1.00, leadership was forced to rethink their growth strategy and ask what the "repeatable keys" to success were. They concluded that the company could build on its core glass technology, a deep appreciation of customer problems, and a willingness to take big but well understood risks. Its biggest opportunity was based on a manufacturing process it had originally developed for auto windshields, but that could be applied to the glass substrates for flat LCD displays. This "Gorilla Glass" technology was extended to cell phones initially, then to laptops and desktop monitors, and onward to TVs and ever larger displays.

Corning Glass represents the payoff that can be achieved from an imaginative integration of outside-in and inside-out thinking, when fueled by advances in technology. The key, of course, is to start from the outside in to expand the mind-set, and thereby avoid the dangers of inside-out myopia that emphasize gaining maximum returns from existing assets and capabilities.

This integrated approach helps explain how James Dyson transformed vacuum cleaners. Consumers had every right to be frustrated with the way their upright units quickly lost suction. The reason was that disposable bags became clogged with dirt particles. This was an obvious design flaw, and yet vacuum cleaners had been made that way for a century. After much experimentation, Dyson found the solution in a novel design that used powerful centrifugal force to separate the dirt from the air. While this may seem like an idea that should have been implemented decades ago, it was in fact enabled by relatively new advances in the formulation of polycarbonate plastics.

Figure 1-5
Integrating Outside-In and Inside-Out Thinking

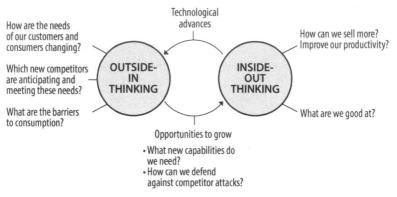

Adjacencies: The Sweet Spot for Profitable Growth

While small-*i* projects are necessary for continuous improvement, they don't give companies a competitive edge or contribute much to profitability. It's the moves into adjacent markets and beyond that generate the profits needed to close the growth gap.

Adjacencies achieve a better balance of risk and reward by striking into new territory while drawing on the resources and market knowledge of the business. A market adjacency has some similarity to the currently served market in that the firm's brand promise and customer relationships have some relevance in the new market, and distribution and sales activities partially overlap. For instance, USAA found a profitable adjacency among the relatives of military members. (Members of the armed forces were their original market.) There will also be some similarities in the competitors in adjacent markets so competitive moves can be better anticipated. An adjacency on the product/technology dimension has some overlap with the company's value chain, technology and manufacturing competency, quality standards, and so forth, and helps the firm leverage its knowledge base.

Most firms steer clear of very risky BIG-*I* initiatives that take the business beyond adjacencies, to the point where there is no connection to the current business. Growth leaders fuel their sustained growth by carefully sequencing their adjacency moves; first understanding and containing the risk by proximal moves, then building on the expanded base to move toward more distant adjacencies. Seldom do they make a move into more distant, disconnected markets in one jump. Otis, the elevator maker, started with elevators and spare parts; then expanded into services such as financing, maintenance, and intelligent monitoring; and then, with that knowledge and market credibility, moved into service contracts and "build, maintain, and operate" contracts. Successful adjacencies create new platforms for growth, or as Sun Tzu once said, "The more opportunities I seize, the more opportunities multiply before me."

Developing a Strategic Posture

The next step is to decide how you will go about the search for growth opportunities that will close the growth gap. Unfortunately, this part of the growth strategy is the least likely to be made explicit. You can think of your strategic posture as a three-legged stool that reflects your stance on dispositions toward how to grow. Each leg represents a strategic preference: build, buy, or both; open versus closed; inventor versus imitator. These are not binary choices. A continuum exists in each of these areas—but this spectrum makes it all the more important to clarify your firm's posture.

The choices and their rationales need to be spelled out so everyone on the management team can understand, probe, and question whether they are the best choices for the future. The payoff is better organizational alignment, fewer misunderstandings, and better decisions.

Build, Buy, or Both?

There are myriad ways to grow the top and bottom lines of a company or a business unit. Our focus is on *organic growth*, achieved through the innovation prowess of the organization.

This kind of growth is "organic" because it comes from within and is realized with the resources, ingenuity, and focused energy of the organization.

Inorganic growth, from the acquisition of an existing firm with an established record of revenues and profits, is always an option. Buying another company can jump-start entry into an unfamiliar and risky new market; quickly provide access to the skills needed to use a new technology; and expand channel and geographic coverage. A small acquisition can give a toehold in a new industry from which to learn the realities of unfamiliar terrain. Acquisitions are a risky option, however, as the anticipated financial returns often don't materialize.[15] Eager buyers are prone to pay too much for the acquisition, and are often overly optimistic about their ability to integrate the people, processes, and technology. Culture clashes may trigger employee attrition.

While organic growth takes longer, it usually yields better risk-adjusted economic returns. While it seems counterintuitive, organic growth is usually cheaper. If a company has a track record of consistent organic growth, the stock market can reasonably expect it to continue, and will give the firm a higher price-to-earnings ratio. At the same time, there is less debt to support, and the organization is less stressed. As the firm builds new technology and deeper, better capabilities and gains insights into opportunities in adjacent markets, it has a more stable platform on which to continue to grow.

Mutually Reinforcing Approaches to Growth

It is simplistic and counterproductive to frame the best route to growth as a choice between organic (make) versus inorganic (buy). The real issue is finding the right balance so the two are complementary. This begins by thinking of building and buying as end points for a continuum of possibilities, as in Figure 1-6.

Savvy firms make investments at every point along this continuum. Cisco, for example, adroitly combines each of these mechanisms to drive its growth.[16] At the "build" end of the continuum it has 20,000 company engineers working on extending

Figure 1-6
The Organic–Inorganic Growth Continuum

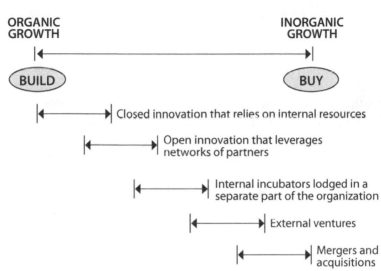

and improving its current products or developing the next generation. These people often work in open networks with external partners to access new technologies or market concepts. It may otherwise take too long to build the internal capabilities. For breakthrough or disruptive innovations that are beyond the company's capabilities, it has created an internal incubator called the Emerging Technology Group, with direct line reporting to the CEO. The budget of this group is carefully protected in good times and bad. On average about four out of nine of these internally incubated innovations succeed. The company also invests heavily in small start-up ventures working on new applications or next-generation technologies that offer new avenues for growth. Cisco takes a small initial ownership stake in these external ventures, and supports them with engineering experts and market insights. If a start-up venture succeeds, it may buy the portion of the company it doesn't own and "spin in" the once-separate start-up. Finally, it is an active acquirer of going concerns.

Open, Closed, or Blended?

Few firms use completely open innovation processes, relying on partners for key activities, or on fully closed processes where everything is done within the confines of the organization. The closed or vertically integrated model prevailed through the 1980s but lost favor as firms opening their innovation process scored impressive gains in the quality of their ideas, access to technology, and time to market. A further impetus came from the recognition that important innovations emerge from small and medium-size firms willing to license or sell their intellectual property. Today the possibilities of open innovation have blossomed along with the Internet. Now it is much easier to connect with outside resources through a variety of mechanisms, ranging from innovation contests to dedicated open-innovation service providers such as InnoCentive.

The choice to be open is not simply a matter of bolting on a few R&D partners, taking stakes in early-stage companies, or posting a prize on the Internet. Open innovation takes a change in mind-set to enable giving up a degree of the control that comes with ownership. While you must cede some ownership, it is possible for a partner outside the bounds of the firm to be closely coordinated.

The shift from closed to open innovation was accelerated by the success of Proctor & Gamble's "Connect + Develop" model.[17] This was an explicit recognition that for every P&G researcher, there were 200 scientists or engineers who were just as good in their areas, and that, historically, many of P&G's best ideas had come from teams working across division boundaries. Top management support for this move was crucial, capped by CEO A. G. Lafley, who set a goal that half the company's future new products would come from partners.

There is no right or wrong answer to the question of how far the innovation process should be opened—but the management team has to take a position. To gain an advantage and preempt competitors—who are attracted by the same logic drawing you to the opportunity—the firm has to be prepared to invest in partnering skills, including the ability to find the best partners, and in aligning activities and incentives across boundaries. We will dissect these skills and capabilities further in Chapter 4.

First Mover, Fast Follower, or Imitator?

The third leg of the posture stool is the orientation toward pioneering to be a first mover versus waiting and then imitating. This is a variation on the classic strategic choice of exploration versus exploitation. When a new market opportunity emerges, the players whose scope potentially includes this opportunity have to decide whether to enter first, with the hope of establishing the dominant design and preempting competition, or to watch and wait until the fog of uncertainty is partially lifted.

Pioneers are willing to accept much more risk, and invest in early stage R&D capabilities to gain a technological advantage and generate a flow of opportunities. These trailblazers have to prove the innovation works, invest to create and grow the market, and then fend off rivals. This posture is frequently adopted by early-stage start-ups, often in the hope of exiting with an IPO or being acquired by a deep-pocketed company.

A variation on the pure pioneering posture is the conscious decision to be a fast second.[18] These are often established firms whose core business could be jeopardized by a new technology or business model. While it may not be in their interest for the innovation to become established, it is certainly in their interest to become a leader in the new market once it emerges. Firms that adopt a fast-second posture have little incentive to move first, so they ready themselves to move as soon as there is an indication that the innovation is gaining traction. To consistently succeed, they must have mastered the new technology (perhaps with an open-innovation approach) and have a product and business model ready to go, plans for manufacturing or sourcing in place, and a marketing strategy that specifies how they will attack the emerging market. To follow a fast-second strategy, a firm must be prepared to do everything a first mover does—which includes having a highly developed market-sensing capability—while continuing to drive its core business forward and watching to see if the market for the innovation shows signs of taking off.

An alternative to being a fast second is adopting an imitative posture. This means accepting smaller rewards with less risk by capitalizing—with a strong brand, unique market access, or a low-cost production advantage—on the opportunities created by the pioneer. Successful imitators are adroit at identifying unserved niches. This doesn't have to be a "me too" strategy, which offers little incentive for the customers to switch unless prices are slashed. "Innovative imitators" may understand the customers better and see the possibilities for meaningful improvements that add customer value. Thus Green Mountain Coffee Roasters innovatively imitated the sophisticated and expensive single-serving coffeemakers from Europe, with a simpler and cheaper business model innovation. Their Keurig machine followed a razor-razorblade approach by selling machines cheaply and making money on disposable cups of coffee of an acceptable quality.

Allocating Resources

The fastest way to subvert an ambitious growth strategy is not to allocate enough money or people right now to close an impending growth gap. It takes time to build new organizational capabilities and develop and launch growth initiatives before they start to generate revenue and throw off cash. If adequate resources are not allocated, key implementers get the message that senior management is not committed to the strategy or the growth objectives, and return to business as usual.

The pivotal decision is how much to spend on small-*i* innovations to protect the core business, versus longer payback investments in organic growth from adjacencies and BIG(ger)-*I* initiatives. This choice cannot be avoided, and it is better to approach it mindfully by considering the following questions:[19]

- How much, and what kind of growth will come from acquisitions? Many companies choose to buy their way into places beyond their core, with learning investments into small start-ups or takeovers of established players. The answer to this question depends on availability, with high-technology sectors such as biopharmaceuticals spawning lots of candidates.

• How much growth will come from the momentum of the current strategy? If the momentum is expected to stall, then more resources will have to allocated to adjacencies and BIG-*I* opportunities. A related consideration is whether the company is the market leader, and eager to protect its position, or a niche player content to retreat to a smaller position.

• What does our industry structure permit us to do? Here the binding constraints include the maturity of the served market, the capital intensity of the business, and the robustness of intellectual property protection. Thus, the fast-growing mobile communications sector supports many more opportunities for growth from technology innovation than the staid consumer food products sector, where most innovations are incremental line extensions, feature upgrades, and other small-*i* innovations.

• How experienced is the business in bringing significant growth initiatives to market? If the business has a strong growth culture, well-honed capabilities, and a proven track record, it can comfortably commit a larger allocation of resources to riskier adjacencies and BIG-*I* projects.

The larger point is that each company settles on an allocation ratio that reflects its aspirations and capabilities. There is no magic formula that works for everyone. However, a recent study[20] found that growth leaders converge around the following allocation:

70% to their core business for small-*i* innovation (in some formulations, called the near-term Horizon One);

20% to adjacencies (Horizon Two); and

10% to BIG-*I* innovations (also called transformational or disruptive Horizon Three initiatives).

The study claimed that this breakdown was correlated with a meaningfully higher share price performance across many industries. While a full measure of skepticism is warranted, it is nonetheless a good departure point for an internal debate about whether the current allocation is right. A corollary debate will quickly ensue over the sources of funding for each category. Each business unit can and should fund small-*i* innovations and perhaps even close-in adjacencies from its own cash flow as part of the annual budget cycle. The controversy always arises over funding riskier adjacencies and BIG-*I* initiatives. The business units will resent and resist a corporate innovation tax on their budgets, because they won't see how they will benefit. For these riskier undertakings, the funding should come out of a corporate innovation fund that is separate from business unit profit-and-loss control. Proctor & Gamble's experience here is instructive and sobering. Between 2003 and 2008 the business unit heads were given primary responsibility for innovation, which tied research spending to their shorter-term profit concerns. According to Bruce Brown, P&G's chief technology officer, by 2010 the number of big-product breakthroughs fell to an average of fewer than six per year as small-*i* innovations got more attention and resources.[21]

Guidance for Managers: Test Your Growth Strategy

In this chapter, I've offered a template, based on best practices, for the design of a growth strategy that can both energize and focus your organization. The elements in the template cannot be ignored—because they shape how a firm approaches innovation and makes choices. You must have an open dialogue about these choices, rather than let them be tacit and unexamined. To bring the key elements into the open, the management team should ask a series of probing and instructive questions:

- How many members of the top management team agree with the growth objectives and are confident they can be reached?
- What are the pivotal assumptions underlying the momentum strategy and choice of objectives, and how solid is the supporting evidence?

- Will the growth initiatives in the opportunity portfolio close the anticipated growth gap?
- Is there a consensus on the choice of scope and posture? Will the parent company endorse these choices?
- What has been the track record with acquisitions? When have acquisitions been disappointing versus successful? What can be done to improve the success rate?
- How do our capabilities for identifying, valuing, and integrating acquisitions compare with those of our direct rival or potential entrant?
- Are we ahead of or behind our rivals in building an open-innovation capability and in lining up the best development, technology, and marketing partners?
- Is our array of opportunities better suited to a pioneering, fast-second, or imitative posture? What does our heritage and management DNA say about which posture we should adopt?
- What is our allocation of people and financial resources for protecting the core, versus growing into adjacencies, versus implementing a high-risk BIG-*I* innovation? How does this allocation compare with that of our rivals? What allocation ratio is needed to close the growth gap?

Chapter 2

Expand the Search for Growth Opportunities

F ew firms lack ideas to pursue. A reactive approach will sweep up a lot of possibilities: R&D will envision new features, performance enhancements, and technologies; distributors, salespeople, and employees will suggest new products; there will be pressure to match or leapfrog a competitor by copying and adapting its innovations; and changes in strategy will require (and inspire) supporting innovations. While these sources of ideas should always be encouraged, the odds of coming up with a great idea by waiting and reacting are much lower than if there is a directed search.

A directed search for opportunities that thoroughly covers the full scope of the growth strategy, will surface better-quality ideas earlier than will simply waiting for such opportunities to emerge. If the competitor sees an idea sooner, it is much harder to gain an advantage. The benefits will be further lessened if the search is confined to familiar places, where most of the development activity has been focused in the past.

To combat the narrowing forces of habit, I have created a full-spectrum innovation approach, composed of 14 growth pathways. These pathways allow firms to stretch, push, and reimagine every dimension of their strategy, including the customer value proposition and the business model.[22]

Full-Spectrum Innovation

DuPont has been making sulfuric acid since 1865, from the days when it supplied John D. Rockefeller's first oil refinery with barrels of acid delivered on horse-drawn wagons. This is a slow-growth, price-competitive market—surely a profit wasteland. So why is DuPont still in the business? Because it found a major growth opportunity with a service for efficiently regenerating spent sulfuric acid. Spent sulfuric acid is highly valued by petroleum refiners, which have to use more acid to process high-sulfur crude while reducing their emissions. DuPont builds, owns, operates, and maintains sulfuric acid production facilities within gasoline refiners' plants that not only regenerate the refiners' spent acid but also capture the acid gas emissions. This success story set in an ultra-mature chemicals market displays the main features of the full-spectrum innovation approach in action, while also demonstrating the truth of the old saying that there is no such thing as a commodity—only commodity thinking.

Much of the discussion about innovation today focuses on a narrow set of ideas around design and functionality. Such innovations capture attention because they are obvious even to casual observers. The iPod or Kindle, for instance, did something no other product could do, and looked different from every other product on the market when launched. But such a view of innovation is far too narrow—and constrains the growth efforts of too many firms. A major factor in developing innovation prowess is breaking out of this narrow range of thinking and searching for valuable innovations—and therefore growth—along the full spectrum of possibilities.

Before thinking about the full spectrum of innovation possibilities, it is helpful to think of a firm's participation in a market as made up of two parts: the value the firm provides to customers, and the firm's business model—or, put another way, the firm's value-creating and value-capturing systems. For successful firms, the customer value proposition and the business model are tightly integrated. Tight integration ensures that the firm is able to deliver the value it promises to customers and efficiently capture that value in the form of revenue.

Full-spectrum innovation addresses both sides of this whole. It investigates opportunities to innovate the customer value proposition and innovate the business model. Each of these primary realms can be further subdivided, ultimately leading to 14 distinct pathways for value-generating innovation (see

Figure 2-1). Eight of these pathways fall into the customer value proposition; the remaining six are pathways for innovating the business model.

Figure 2-1
Full-Spectrum Innovation: The 14 Growth Pathways

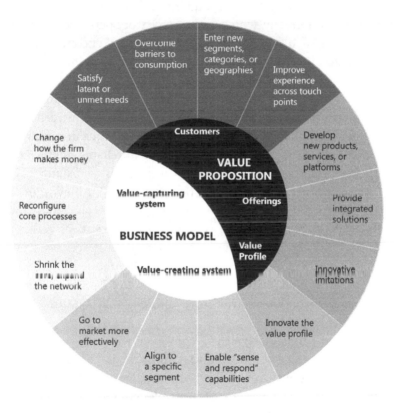

The full-spectrum innovation coin has two sides. On one side is the customer value proposition; on the other is the business model that spells out how the business profitably fulfills the value proposition. Growth pathways can start on either side of the coin, but success requires the two sides to be tightly linked and synchronized.

The power of these linkages can be seen at work in General Electric's successful entry into the global wind turbine market. The first step was a small acquisition in 2003 to learn about the market. The company then leveraged its capabilities in making gas turbines and jet engines to develop a better wind turbine, while challenging the current competitive profile. At the time, the global market was heavily dependent on government subsidies, especially in Germany, which has a scarcity of open land. German competitors, such as Siemens, responded to market conditions by offering 20 different models that could fit on different-size plots of land.

Deep immersion into the needs of current and prospective customers revealed two main drivers of customers' perceptions of economic value: gearbox reliability and efficiency in capturing wind energy. Existing wind turbines were unreliable, inefficient, and costly because of short production runs. These insights gave GE the confidence to challenge the prevailing business model. It began investing heavily in improving turbine efficiency and reliability. To reach scale, it offered only one size of turbine, one that met the needs of markets where tight spaces were not a constraint. With design changes and high-volume production, GE improved reliability (uptime) from 85% to 97%. GE also drew on aircraft technologies to design turbines that captured 20% more wind energy.

Each growth pathway can be combined with other pathways, in myriad ways. The reach and ambition of the innovation along each pathway can range from small-*i* thinking to BIG-*I* breakthroughs. The variety of possible combinations can be daunting, but also encouraging. Markets reward a value-adding variety of growth initiatives—offering grounds for optimism for any firm whose growth is lagging. It is unlikely that all the best combinations have been exploited. The challenge is not a lack of attractive pathways but finding the energy and imagination to systematically pursue them ahead of rivals.

The Customer Value Proposition Growth Pathways

The customer value proposition is made up of three distinct areas: a definition of the customers being served; the details of the product being offered; and a comparison of the value offered by the product with alternatives. Innovation can proceed in any of these three areas.

Customer Pathway

Growth is often the result of expanding the served market arena. Most market definitions are artificial constructs, so an outside-in approach challenges these boundaries by asking two questions: What other needs of our current customers can we serve? What other customers could use our capabilities? This is the antithesis of pursuing market share.

Offerings Pathway

Offerings that create superior customer value are often found at the intersection of technology advances and customer needs. For instance, in the field of cardiac surgery, there was an enormous need for an arterial stent that could open arteries and not cause problems years after insertion. Abbott Laboratories responded by developing a stent made of bioabsorbable plastic that simply dissolves into the bloodstream within a year or two after its work of opening an artery is done, similar to the way sutures or bone screws are ultimately absorbed. This stent is a huge boon to customers, who no longer have to worry about stent thrombosis— the rare but fatal clotting caused by stents that stay in blood vessels years after being inserted—and a source of organic growth for Abbott. There are other ways to innovate offerings beyond introducing new technologies, such as providing integrated solutions that add value to existing offerings or tweaking aspects of existing innovations.

Value Profile Pathway

The final pathway for innovating the value proposition is to change the value profile of an offering. In most product categories, a conventional wisdom develops about the acceptable range of price to value. Innovating the value profile involves challenging this conventional wisdom in various ways.

The Business Model Growth Pathways

The term *business model* suggests a complex and abstract representation. Good business models are anything but abstract. A good business model addresses two enduring issues:[23]

1. **Value-creating system.** What business activities are neces-sary to create the value we promise our customers?
2. **Value-capturing system.** How do we make money while creat-ing value for our customers?

The business model pathways are broken down into two subgroups accordingly: value-creating pathways and value-capturing pathways.

Business model innovations are generally more profitable than customer value innovations. IBM found that companies with above-average profit margin growth allocated 50% more to business model innovation than did underperforming companies.[24] These profit gains are sustainable because significant business model innovations require rearranging many linked activities that are hard for competitors to understand or copy. Such innovations may also create a versatile platform on which a stream of value proposition innovations can be generated.

This discussion of pathways in the business model category is more suggestive than comprehensive. Each pathway can be creatively combined with other pathways in myriad ways that could never be described exhaustively. The key when exploring business model pathways is to ensure that you are asking questions that probe every assumption and construct of your current business model in terms both of value creation and of value capture.

The 14 Growth Pathways

In the rest of this chapter, I'll go into more detail on each of the 14 growth pathways of full-spectrum innovation. Each pathway will be described in detail with relevant examples. As you read about each of the pathways, consider whether your firm has used this pathway to innovate new customer value in the last three years. If not, consider what organic growth opportunities you have left on the table.

Pathway 1: Satisfy latent or unmet needs

The foundation for this pathway is deep insights that generate a novel understanding of the customer. Campbell's Soup used these insights success- fully to enter the Russian market in 2007. Campbell's had learned that soup played a deep and com- plex role in the hearts and stomachs of Russian men. The firm's researchers found that, in a typical Russian home, it was very 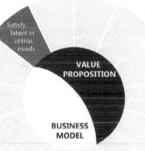 common for a pot of meat bones to be boiling on the kitchen stove. Russian wives would spend several days nurturing the rich broth and recovering large chunks of meat and savory fats. This process, Russians believed, puts the *dousha*, or soul, into the soup. Given this context, bringing ready-made soup into this market was not going to be easy. Several competitors had tried to enter with Western European bagged and premixed soups. Russian women scoffed, and Russian men considered the use of such products unacceptable. These ready-to-serve soups "had no soul."

As the purveyors of this *dousha*, however, Russian women were in a bind. Since they worked full time, they could not tend to the soup that had such importance in the Russian household. This was the customers' problem—and Campbell's opportunity. Through a process of ethnographic work involving deep interactions with Russian families, Campbell's developed a product that could offer Russian women a way to solve the problem of preparing homemade soup with packaged ingredients. The Domashnaya Klassika ("Home Classics") line of soup contains large chunks of meat and visible fat medallions. To a Western eye it looks unfinished. To Russian eyes, it looks authentic and homemade.

The Campbell's approach exemplifies the robust outside-in innovation process applied by the design firm IDEO to develop new offerings (Figure 2-2).

Figure 2-2
The IDEO Development Process

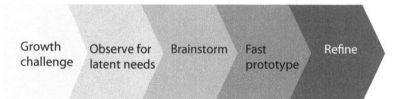

We will revisit the IDEO process later, but I highlight here the central role of observational or ethnographic methods. The core idea is that latent needs are "evident but not yet obvious." They require skilled observers who can immerse themselves in the target customer's world. Many other tools can be used to extract deep customer insights with a directed search, including in-depth interviews, problem identification and metaphor-elicitation methods, and customer experience maps.[25] To hear the voice of the customer, firms can also try these methods:

- **Leverage lead users.** These are users who face needs in advance of the rest of the market, and are working to find a solution sooner. Products such as correction fluid, sports bras, and Gatorade came from lead users (professional typists and elite athletes, respectively). In categories such as construction equipment or scientific test instruments, most innovation ideas come from alterations to products or workarounds made by lead users.

- **Monitor complainers and defectors.** Myopia about customers can be combated by learning from unhappy customers, who express frustration when their needs are not met or understood.
- **Hunt for precursors in the parts of the country or globe where fads, fashions, or technology innovations tend to appear earlier.** Companies such as the footwear-maker Converse have used "cool hunters" and trend trackers as an early warning radar, to uncover trends such as the rise of retro in clothing and shoes.
- **Anticipate consequences of supportive trends.** FedEx has found opportunities in "global components handling" enabled by trends in globalized freight flows, outsourcing demands, and Internet availability. Trends may emerge from fringe markets and extend outward. Thus, snowboarding, microbrewers, and extreme sports have become popular with mainstream markets.

Pathway 2: Overcome barriers to consumption

The Nintendo Wii home video game console broke the record for the bestselling console in a single month by appealing to non-consumers of video games. As Satoru Iwata, the CEO of Nintendo, said, "We are not competing against Sony PlayStation or Microsoft's Xbox. We are battling the indifference of people who have no interest in video games."

Nintendo overcame this indifference by challenging industry conventional wisdom and simplifying rather than adding power and complexity, making game play more physically active (and therefore recognizable to non-gamers), designing a user-friendly controller, and reducing the price barrier with a launch price of $250 (versus PS3's $599).

Nonconsumers of any particular offering are not necessarily uninterested. Some would consume if they could, but face a barrier that constrains their ability to solve a problem or satisfy a need. Four different kinds of consumption barriers have been identified;[26] overcoming each barrier is a potential growth opportunity:

1. **Lack of money.** Existing alternatives are too expensive.
2. **Lack of skills.** Existing alternatives are complex, requiring expert guidance or lots of training.
3. **Lack of access.** Alternatives can be consumed only in specific contexts, locations, and so on.
4. **Lack of time.** Consumption of alternatives takes too long

Wii overcame the "lack of money" and "lack of skills" barriers by offering an intuitive product that even non-gamers could immediately enjoy, at a significant discount (roughly 30%) to other gaming platforms.

It takes well-honed outside-in thinking, guided by an investment in market insights, to both identify and overcome the barriers to consumption. The solution is often a challenge to existing expertise and embedded mental models about how things should be properly done.

Pathway 3: Enter new segments, categories, or geographies

I could spend the entirety of this chapter discussing new segments or new categories. A great deal has been written on this pathway in the marketing literature, and most senior executives and marketing leaders will be familiar with it. Here, let me just briefly mention an area that presents exciting new innovation opportunities: entering new geographies.

Penetrating new geographies is a compelling growth pathway in an era in which developing countries are major growth engines. Big opportunities are being found at the "base of the pyramid" in these countries, with their vast but individually poor

populations. This prospect is very
tempting to Procter & Gamble.
The logic is simple: Americans
spend about $110 a year per
capita on P&G products. The
worldwide per capita figure
is $12. Sales in Mexico are
$20 a year per capita, with
sales in China and India between $1 and $3 per year per
capita. P&G's aim is to get the
per capita numbers in China and
India closer to those of Mexico.

Recently the presumption that innovations developed for
the demanding markets of the United States, Europe, and Japan
will, with some adaptation, also meet the needs of rapidly
developing countries has been challenged on two fronts. First,
stripped-down versions are not enough; consumers in developing
countries respond when offerings meet their unique needs.
Second, innovations focused on developing-market customers
are increasingly proving to be appealing to developed-country
consumers interested in simplicity, ease of use, or energy
efficiency. The traditional flow of innovation from rich to poor
countries is starting to move in reverse.[27]

Pathway 4: Improve the customer experience across all touch points

Every purchase decision by a customer, from installing a
medical device to choosing and staying at a hotel, has a distinct
beginning, middle, and end, with many steps along the way that
take place over time. The key is to capture the complete customer
experience from the customer's perspective—not what you hoped
or expected the customer to experience of your offering. The
generic process outlined in Figure 2-3 is evocative; the process
is often more convoluted, leading to many opportunities for
innovative reimagining.

Once the steps are mapped, new customer value can be created by asking yourself which steps in the process pre-sent opportunities for improvement:

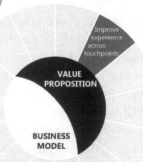

- Which steps can be improved? Westin Hotels created the "Heavenly Experience" after interviews and observations of people getting ready for bed revealed the priority that business travelers gave to a good night's sleep.
- Which steps can be eliminated, combined in a different sequence, or made smarter? Can the burden be automated, or shifted elsewhere?
- Where are the pain points?
- What factors dictate who gets included in the consideration set?
- Where can time delays be eliminated?

With an outside-in view of what the customer sees, hears, feels, and does, companies can improve their existing offering or find white space opportunities. The key is to rethink all points of contacts, even the prosaic ones. American Girl and Cabela's outdoor stores have turned their storefronts into destinations. Whether you're having an ice-cream sundae with your doll at the "parlor" (American Girl) or taking rifle practice near a waterfall (Cabela's), these stores do much more than just provide access to merchandise and helpful sales people. They reinforce and differentiate the value of their products.

Figure 2-3
Customer Experience Mapping

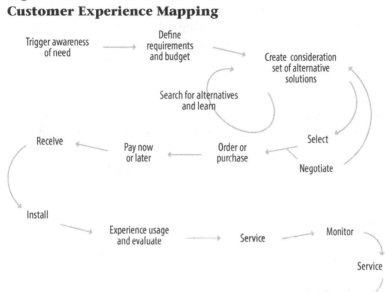

Pathway 5: Develop innovative new products, services, or platforms

This pathway is more like an auto-bahn or expressway for most companies—it is a wide pathway that absorbs most resources. Consequently, it is generally the best managed of the innovation activities, with guidance from tools such as stage gating, and real-options investments. The focus is on the application of new knowledge and technology developments, put in new combina-

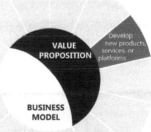

tions that add value to customers. (Think of GPS systems or ABS braking.) This pathway is most productive when it is guided by deep insights into latent or unsatisfied needs.

The technology base for this pathway can be either sustaining or disruptive to the business. A *disruptive* technology has the potential to invalidate existing advantages, and is hard for an incumbent to match because it would compromise existing resources. This is especially a risk when the established technology is complex and costly relative to a disruptive technology that is cheaper and simpler while good enough to meet the needs of most customers. Salesforce.com disrupted the market for customer relationship management (CRM) software. The incumbents, such as SAP, sold high-priced enterprise software customized to the customer, and charged high fees for installation. Salesforce.com sold software as a service, and rented access to programs in the "cloud" (i.e., they resided on centralized host computers). These programs were easy to use and much cheaper than the incumbents' offering, which suited most medium-size and small customers. While disruptive technologies get a lot of attention— because they change the status quo—most technology advances are of the *sustaining* variety; incumbents can adopt them without undercutting their value proposition.

Two important variants on this product growth pathway are broad design and platform innovations. A platform is a set of modular components that serve as the building blocks of a family of products or services. With these modules, a diverse set of offerings can be created more rapidly and cheaply than designing each one separately. Microsoft Windows is a platform that enabled the creation of many derivative programs and services, ranging from Office to Windows Phone to technician certifications.

Design innovation seeks to create products with appearance and functionality that make them instantly recognizable. The emphasis here is on creativity, often expressed through high-quality and artistic form factors. This is the essence of Bang & Olufsen, the Danish maker of TVs, sound systems, telephones, and other electronic devices. New ideas, materials, and technologies made their way into B&O products when designers put them there, and engineers then had to find ways to make them at scale.

Pathway 6: Provide integrated solutions

A true solution is an integrated bundle of products and related services that creates value for the customer that is more than the sum of its parts. Such a solution meets four criteria:

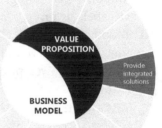

1. It is co-created with customers.
2. It is tailored to each customer's requirements.
3. It delivers superior service on the customer's terms, including rapid response, ready access, and clear accountability from the supplier.
4. Some of the risk perceived by customers is absorbed by suppliers through performance- or risk-based contracts or commitments.

It's easy simply to label a bundle that enables one-stop shopping as a "solution." But such solutions are not valuable innovations. Competitors can copy them easily, and so they do not typically result in growth. Growth comes from solutions based on an outside-in insight into how to solve a customer's problems. True solutions help customers succeed on their terms. One excellent example of this type of innovation is GE's and Rolls-Royce's "power by the hour" programs, which allow customers to pay a fixed fee per hour of usage of an aircraft engine, which gives customers much greater cost certainty.

Pathway 7: Innovative imitation

Imitations often can become winners, but they have to do more than just copy. The key is to understand the appeal of the original innovation, and the barriers to its success, with an eye to making improvements in ways customers value. Thus, the iPod was not the first digital music player, and the iPhone was not the first smartphone. Apple took the originators' concepts and made them far more appealing. The multibillion-dollar category of own-label, or private label, products is based on copying well-known brands but at a much lower price point for the same quality. Fast-fashion firms such as ZARA have prospered by copying designs from the catwalk and

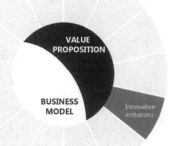

getting them onto hangers in retail stores far faster than competitors (or even the original designers).

Followers usually lower R&D costs, and face less risk of failure because the product concept has already been market tested. To win, they need to learn fast from the pioneer's problems and deploy a flexible organization that can move fast to develop a superior version before the competition is inspired to follow. Another way for an innovative imitator to win is to unleash a much larger go-to-market capability and cover the market more thoroughly.

Pathway 8: Innovate the value profile

This pathway focuses on how to gain a competitive advantage by challenging industry conventional wisdom. It works best in tandem with other pathways because it usually requires a new offering and a rethinking of the target segment. The starting point is a profile of the different level of product (or service) features offered by competitors. Innovations

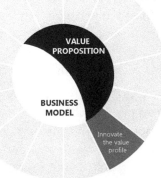

come from challenging these profiles,[27] by asking which features can be eliminated, increased, reduced, or added for the product to be below or above the industry standard. The value profile should include all the factors (beyond the product itself) that customers use when making a choice.

This was the approach used to design the Ginger budget hotel chain, launched in India in 2004 by the Tata Group (which also runs the Taj hotel chain). The chain was designed to meet the needs of frequent business travelers who wanted a place to stay that was not as earthy or as unpredictable as a low-price hotel, but who could not pay the sky-high prices of a five-star hotel.

The Ginger brand promises a customer experience that is "consistent, simple, light-hearted" at the best price. The small rooms are strictly no-frills, with dorm-style furniture, but with state-of-the-art new mattresses. Costs are tightly controlled by locating the hotels in business districts, away from high-cost real estate, and using self-check-in and minimal staff. The resulting competitive profile (shown in Figure 2-4) clearly sets Ginger apart from the competing hotels and aligns the hotel with the needs of its target segment.

Figure 2-4
The Budget Hotel Market in India

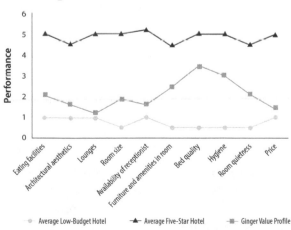

Source: Published materials, site visits, and hotel reviews.

Pathway 9: Enable "sense and respond" capabilities

The essence of this business model pathway is the modularization of activities and processes to create combinations of products that are responsive to unpredictable customer requests. Dell Computer was an early success with its build-to-order model; prospective buyers could design exactly the PC or laptop they wanted, get a price and delivery quote, and place an order all at the same

time. By contrast, "make and sell" firms schedule their operations according to forecasts of likely demand.

A hybrid approach uses a flexible backbone that offers low-cost support and messaging for some customers and deep collaboration and precise tailoring of offers for other customers. Adaptability is provided by front-end LEGO-like modules that are responsive to individual customer's requirement for augmentation, technical support, education, and logistics. Advances in system integration, data analytics, and knowledge-sharing networks help overcome the daunting coordination issues.

Pathway 10: Align to a specific segment

In 2002, Dow Corning, the global leader in silicone-based products, faced a major threat to its business model of providing high-end design services, personalized sales support, and flexibility to its buyers. A price-sensitive buyer was asking for high quality, reliability, and lower price for the standardized items it was buying. This opened the market to low-cost offshore competitors.

To win back the low end of the market, the company built a low-cost model tailored to the needs of the price-sensitive segment, within a new organization called XIAMETER. Sales and distribution costs were slashed by eliminating technical service, lengthening lead times from hours to days, and limiting order-size flexibility and custom handling. The company benefited from a scalable online ordering system, with all communication done solely by e-mail. This new model was enabled by deep market insights that

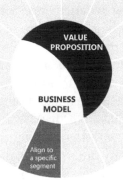

showed that 70% of the market still had needs aligned with the high-touch sales model.

Pathway 11: Go to market more effectively

Nike's CEO recently explained that "Connecting [with customers] used to be, 'Here's some product and here's some advertising; we hope you like it'...Connecting today is a dialogue."[29] This view explains Nike's shift in its marketing efforts to the digital realm: Print and TV spending is down 40% in just three years. Instead,

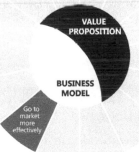

Nike's money is going to online activities, social media, and to supporting communities of users with common interests. To be sure, some of this helps to insulate Nike from the celebrity endorsements gone wrong that have become so common to our era. But it also delivers meaningful customer value by improving the customer's (be he a runner, basketball player, or couch potato) experience, and keeps Nike ahead of rivals.

There is potential for growth-enhancing innovation in every marketing action a firm takes to reach, persuade, and fulfill customer requirements. Some of these innovations respond to the growing complexity of customer solutions and the need to rethink the role of a traditional sales force in an era of ubiquitous access to detailed information. Other innovations respond to cost pressures, to more demanding and connected customers, and to global competition. In the pharmaceutical industry, the traditional model had armies of sales reps fanning out to "detail" doctors with tightly scripted sales pitches on a specific (patent-protected) drug. Multiple sales reps from the same company would call on the same doctor. But doctors today have less time, and even less patience, for such sales pitches—there is less product innovation for the reps to trumpet and growing attention from the public and regulators to the influence of salespeople on doctors' decisions regarding prescribing medication.

In response, some firms are asking their reps to act more like resources to doctors and medical practices. This requires innovations in how drug reps are motivated and evaluated; one firm no longer uses number of prescriptions written as a metric for salespeople, focusing instead on doctor satisfaction. As with Nike, the new focus is on entering into a dialogue with the doctors and addressing their concerns.

Pathway 12: Shrink the core, expand the network[30]

A firm is embedded in a value chain of sequential activities, linked to channels for reaching the market. With each activity, the product gains some value, but the way the chain is designed and managed should create more economic and customer

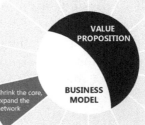

value than the sum of its parts. Advances in coordination devices and information technology have opened up many avenues for innovation by combining activities, shrinking the core of the firm by outsourcing to a network. The aim is to lower costs and increase efficiency. This is how Medco rose to number three (after Nike and Apple) on the list of the most innovative companies in the United States. Essentially Medco reinvented the way people buy medicine by promoting mail-order delivery of drugs and getting doctors and pharmacies to accept electronic delivery of prescriptions. Medco creates value for companies by reducing drug costs for their health plans. As another example, Bharti Airtel became the largest mobile phone company in India by limiting its core activities to customer care, marketing, and the regulatory interface—and outsourcing the rest of the activities.

Pathway 13: Reconfigure core processes

There are abundant opportunities to reimagine how the organization delivers new value to customers. Thus ING Direct Banking of Australia was able to reduce the turnaround time for opening and qualifying the credit worthiness of a new bank account from two days to 15 minutes. The ZARA apparel chain, pioneer of

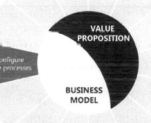

the "fast-fashion" concept, totally rethought its design and manufacturing processes. At most clothing makers the value-creation process starts with designers, who plan collections as much as a year in advance, and requires long lead times and manufacturing in Asia to contain costs. At ZARA, by contrast, fashion and sales trends are monitored continuously to guide in-house designers, who fashion what is hot. These designs are sent to company-owned factories in Spain, where just-in-time systems can move a blouse, dress, or coat from the drawing board to a store in less than a month. Because the chain is more attuned to the latest fashion, it can change more often and doesn't have to mark down large inventories.

Pathway 14: Change how the firm makes money

The ultimate business model question is "How will the firm capture the value it provides to customers?"—in baser terms, "How does the company get paid for the value it creates?" There have been drastic changes in many industries in this area over the last few decades; for many firms, these changes have been involuntary. The media industry in general has struggled to innovate 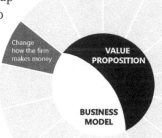 how firms make money in an era of easy downloads and file sharing. While many customers are abandoning the traditional "cable package," neither the firms that produce entertainment (such as HBO) or the firms that deliver it (such as Comcast) have been able to innovate an "à la carte" approach, which customers clearly want, while making enough money to sustain themselves.[31]

The most common form of innovating the value-capture system in recent years has been shifting from a product-sale model to a service model. Today you can lease industrial carpet as easily as a copier. Service models are just about leasing. Praxair captures the increased value of delivering gases right to the point of use in a factory rather than just dropping off a tank car. Castrol Industrial innovated a model to share gains from reduced use of its products based on advice it gave to a client—in other words, the firm now captures increased value by advising its customers on how to buy *less* product.[32] Clearly there are many opportunities for innovation in this pathway.

Conclusion

Curves Fitness Centers became the largest fitness and health club franchise in the world with 4 million members in 2012, by simultaneously innovating the *offering, the target customer segment,* and *the value profile* of the full-service health club. Traditional health clubs catered to men and women and offered a full range of equipment at a high monthly fee. Curves is positioned as a women's gym, providing a total body workout in 30 minutes at one-third the monthly fee. Its equipment is especially designed for women and arranged in a circle to encourage conversation; timed music moves participants from machine to machine in a way that makes the overall experience enjoyable.[33]

Curves has sampled effectively from four of the eight most prevalent value proposition pathways. The main pathway underlying its innovation is the delivery of a different profile of attributes from traditional full-service health clubs. But it also overcomes barriers to consumption among women and, to a lesser degree, satisfies latent or unmet needs for a disciplined workout with social reinforcement. At the same time, its offering is an innovative arrangement of standard elements found in many health clubs. But Curves offers yet a deeper lesson: The more pathways involved with an innovation initiative, the more compelling and integrated the value proposition, and the harder it is for rivals to copy or leapfrog. This doesn't mean competitors won't try to copy Curves, but the odds are that they won't succeed.

Accelerating organic growth once you have settled on a growth strategy is a matter of expanding the search for opportunities, then converging on those that offer the best risk/reward profile. While many organizations have a plethora of risk controls to prevent their wasting time and money on unrealistic possibilities, few take a disciplined approach to pursuing the full spectrum of innovation. By ensuring that your firm is considering all 14 pathways to create new customer value, you can dramatically increase the number of innovation ideas flowing through the firm, therefore boosting the chances you will find opportunities to exploit adjacencies.

Guidance for Managers:
Navigate the Pathways

- Which growth pathway gets the most innovation spending in your industry? Do all competitors behave the same way?
- Where does your business allocate the budget for innovation? How focused or dispersed is your spending (how many different pathways are followed)? What portion of the innovation spending goes to the dominant pathway?
- What portion of your innovation spending is outside the traditional pathways followed by your industry?
- Which pathways have spawned past successful growth initiatives?
- What is the balance of spending on reactive versus directed searches for ideas?
- How effective is your customer insights capability—relative to that of your rivals and to best (next) practices?
- Who is accountable for the portfolio of growth initiatives? What is the process for making resource-allocation decisions? How well understood is this process within the business?

Chapter 3

Converge on the Best Opportunities

A disciplined growth process begins with *divergence*. The aim is to fill the opportunity pipeline by prospecting along the full spectrum of growth pathways. Executed properly, this divergence step in the growth-seeking process will generate far too many possibilities for the business to develop, so the pool of candidates must be pruned by a process of *convergence* on the best opportunities. This chapter describes how to decide which opportunities should be developed. The culmination of convergence is a set of opportunities ready to enter the growth-realization process (which includes, for instance, commercialization) to capture the value created.

Three successively tighter filters are applied to understand and select opportunities that promise the best balance between risk and reward. These filters are generous at first (when uncertainty is high but relatively few resources are at stake), and more aggressive later (when that situation is reversed):

- **Refine the opportunity set.** A particularly useful way to do this is with an "innovation tournament." In a manner similar to the business plan competitions that have become popular in Silicon Valley and at many business schools, opportunities identified by exploring one or more of the growth pathways are pitched to the participants. After discussion, the group decides which opportunities are most interesting and worth further investigation.
- **Screen for learning.** The purpose of this filter is to ensure that all relevant assumptions have been surfaced and tested. This is an exploration of why the winners in the tournament were preferred. Are the underlying assumptions that govern the preferences sound? This filter should identify whether an opportunity warrants further development, needs

additional information before a decision is made, or should be suspended because of a deep flaw that probably can't be fixed.

- **Assess and contain risk.** Finally it is time to decide whether to make a major investment to bring the opportunity to market. Given the uncertainties of market acceptance, competitive responses, and ability to implement, the underlying assumptions need to be revisited, given all that has been learned during the development phase. Do the size of the opportunity and the likelihood of success still justify the costs, taking into account relevant risks? How can these risks be minimized by buying real options?

These three filters overlap—they are asking the same fundamental questions with increasing rigor and intensity. The process of applying them is anything but linear and tidy, despite the summary diagram in Figure 3-1. Instead, there is a messy interplay among the *deliberate* strategic choices that focus on the anticipated opportunity you have chosen to pursue, the unanticipated *emergent* possibilities created from the unexpected problems encountered while trying to implement the original deliberate strategy, and new insights gained from the intense exploration of the market and the technological possibilities.[34]

Refine the Opportunity Set

An innovation tournament is a variation on crowdsourcing, using informed insiders to generate and evaluate a menu of growth opportunities in response to a specific strategic challenge.[35] The advantage of limiting the tournament to insiders is that every participant understands the organic growth challenge, is familiar with the industry, and can be immersed in the research on the growth pathways being explored. While the tournament can be done online, it works better as a one- or two-day in-person workshop to encourage intense strategic dialogue. The strength of the tournament is the ability to help surface and extract exceptional ideas that can garner organizational support.

Figure 3-1
Converge on the Best Opportunities:
Successively Tighter Filters

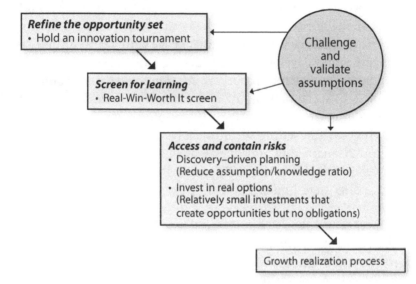

These advantages made an innovation tournament a logical way for a major pharmaceutical company to take a deep dive focused on a growth pathway of "innovating the go-to-market" model. The stakes were high.

Historically, global drug companies were built to discover and commercialize blockbuster drugs that solved the medical problems of millions of people.[36] Think of blood pressure or cholesterol-lowering drugs. By 2012 this business model was in serious jeopardy, as many patents were close to expiring (and hungry generic makers were waiting in the wings); managed care, insurers, and employers were pressing to cut their drug bill; and the drug delivery pipeline had slowed to a trickle at best. The go-to-market approach used by all drug companies relied on armies of well-trained sales reps to "detail," or sell, the drugs to prescribing physicians. This labor-intensive and costly approach was no longer economically justifiable without the steady flow of profits from blockbuster drugs.

The go-to-market model had to be rethought, but there was also a recognition that the sales force was an untapped resource that could drive growth. New roles for salespeople needed to be developed. Instead of just marketing to prescribers, they could target all the relevant players in the health care system, including nurses and pharmacists. They could engage with health insurance companies and develop value-enhancing patient services such as drug-taking compliance programs. All this could take account of advances in social networking and online communications, and perhaps leverage the vast data on prescribing behaviors.

This was the setting for a one-day workshop that included the top 20 marketing and sales managers and a diverse mix of people outside marketing with experience of the market. The participants were immersed in deep background studies on the go-to-market growth pathway, including benchmarking studies, competitor analyses, patient experience maps, and scans of activity on the periphery. There was no shortage of ideas for growth opportunities, but this led to a sort of paralysis, induced by the volume of possibilities and the lack of experience with innovation beyond the launching of new drugs. The objective of the workshop was to energize action, by identifying five to seven significant growth opportunities that fit the growth strategy and leveraged the firm's capabilities. The workshop had two phases, beginning with a divergent generation of growth candidates, followed by an aggressive convergence on a small set of exceptional opportunities.

Generate Growth Ideas

Trial-and-error learning and research on group creativity has produced clear guidelines on how to extract the maximum value from this stage.

Begin by using the insights from the previous chapter to ensure there is a shared understanding of the strategic issues to be addressed. An immersion into customer insights, competitor analyses, precursor market studies, and signals, however weak, from the periphery will ensure that outside-in thinking prevails.

Contrary to popular wisdom, when it comes to generating ideas on how to pursue a growth pathway, individuals are much more productive than the same people brainstorming in a group. The bottleneck created when people speak one at a time, and group dynamics such as groupthink, inhibit the early flow of ideas

Most of the best ideas come from a few people, but it is hard to identify these people in advance. The variability could be due to differences in talent, effort, or understanding of the issues. In general it is better to cast a wider net to ensure that you include these idea generators, rather than narrowing the participants too soon.

The ideation process should encourage the most innovative thinkers to come forward, but be inclusive so that everyone buys into the process and understands the logic of the ideas being proposed, so they will support them later. The approach used by the pharmaceutical firm was to ask each participant to generate growth ideas in 15 minutes. Many were readily conceded to be small-*i* ideas, but these were soon filtered out.

Filter the Growth Ideas

While I'm fond of the funnel metaphor, the innovation process doesn't actually work that way. If it were a funnel, whatever ideas entered at the top would eventually also leave—so the process would be more like prioritization than selection. The aim here is to filter out poorly conceived or inconsequential ideas quickly.

My colleagues at Wharton have devised a number of ways to build a rapid and unbiased consensus around a few big ideas to pursue more thoroughly.[37] In the pharma go-to-market project, there were more than 50 ideas to consider. Each participant was first asked to briefly explain his or her idea. Following these pitch presentations, each idea was described on a flip chart page posted on a wall. Then all the participants were given 10 stickers to allocate to the ideas they believed were best. After the "voting," and a rousing discussion, it was apparent to all that there were only five ideas worth serious consideration. These winners were fleshed out and then subjected to a more rigorous evaluation with the screening methodology described next. This is one example of how to use an innovation tournament. It is a flexible tool, and innovation teams can improvise and adapt it to their needs.

Screen for Learning[38]

The Real-Win-Worth It (R-W-W) screen is a simple but powerful tool built on a series of questions about the innovation concept or product, its potential market, and the company's capabilities and competition. It is not an algorithm for making go/no-go decisions but, rather, a disciplined process that can be employed at multiple stages of product development to expose faulty assumptions, gaps in knowledge, and potential sources of risk, and to ensure that every avenue for improvement has been explored. The R-W-W screen can be used to identify and help fix problems that are weighing on a project, to contain risk, and to expose problems that can't be fixed and therefore should lead to termination of the project.

Innovation is inherently messy, nonlinear, and iterative. For simplicity, we focus on using the R-W-W screen in the early stages, to test the viability of product concepts. In reality, however, a given growth concept would be screened repeatedly during development: at the concept stage, during prototyping, and early in the launch planning. Repeated assessment allows screeners to incorporate increasingly detailed product, market, and financial analyses into the evaluation, yielding ever-more-accurate answers to the screening questions.

R-W-W guides a development team to dig deeply into an idea. Each area of R-W-W breaks down into more detailed questions. At the highest level are three simple questions: Is the idea real? Can we win? Is it worth it? Of course these simple questions are not simple to answer. To enable the search for answers, each of the three high-level questions is broken down further:

Real: *Is the market real? Is the product real?*
Win: *Can the product be competitive? Can our company be competitive?*

Worth It: *Will the product be profitable at an acceptable risk? Does launching the product make strategic sense?*

These questions can then be broken down further. Specific questions are summarized in Figure 3-2 and described in detail in Appendix B.

Figure 3-2
Screening for Success

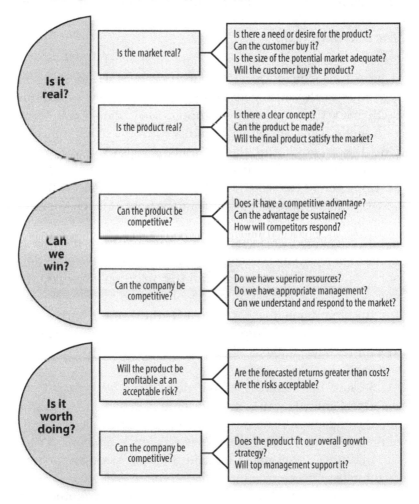

The development team answers these questions by exploring an even deeper set of supporting questions. The team determines where the answer to each question falls on a continuum ranging from "definitely yes" to "definitely no." A definite no to any of the first six fundamental questions typically leads to termination of the project, for obvious reasons. For example, "Can the product be competitive?" If the consensus answer is a definite no, and the team can imagine no way to change it to a yes (or even a maybe), continuing with development would be irrational.

The Screening Team

Project screening teams vary by company, type of initiative, and stage of development. Over the course of R-W-W screening, teams typically involve members from across functions, including R&D, marketing, and manufacturing. They should also work with senior managers who are familiar with the screen and who have the expertise and the instincts to push dispassionately for accurate answers, particularly at each decision point during development. At the same time, however, these managers should be sympathetic and willing to provide the team with the resources to fill in information gaps.

A critical job in managing the R-W-W process is preventing teams from regarding the screening as an obstacle to be overcome or circumvented. It's also important that the team not regard the screening as an arbitrary go/no-go tool imposed by management, and therefore a potential threat to a favorite project. Such a misperception will subvert proper use of the screening as a learning tool for revealing dubious assumptions and identifying problems and solutions.

Because the members of the development team are both evaluators and advocates, the screening is vulnerable to misuse and manipulation. Team members' convictions about the merits of the project may lead them to make cursory evaluations if they fear that a deep assessment, including a frank voicing of doubts, might imperil the project. One way to avoid this pitfall is to enlist a credible outside facilitator, perhaps someone from another part of the company who has a solid new-product track record and no stake in the outcome. This person's job should be to unearth all the key uncertainties, information gaps, and differences of opinion and help resolve them.

Why 3M Embraced R-W-W

One of the most vocal advocates of R-W-W is 3M, where the screening has been used on more than 1,500 projects. The screening's credibility was enhanced when it played a central role in the ultimate success of the company's computer privacy light-control film. Although the company's microlouvered light film, which simulates a tiny venetian blind, promised unique privacy benefits, it almost didn't get to the market. The first two versions failed in market tests, and the sales force was unwilling to carry the finished product because the high sales price threatened to limit sales to a small market niche. At that point it was a technology in search of a market.[39]

A new general manager forced the development team to adopt an outside-in approach, using the R-W-W screen. This revealed that the technology was effective and patent protected, so it couldn't be copied by competitors. However, the R-W-W screening also revealed a complete lack of market knowledge regarding market size and target customer segments, and whether the privacy film would satisfy the most attractive segments. Would they be willing to pay a sufficiently high price? Approval to proceed with development was made contingent on obtaining persuasive evidence of potential demand. This came from test markets; product placements in offices of people with a high need for privacy, such as human resource managers; observational studies; and interviews with computer makers and distributors, which showed a large market potential. Armed with these insights, 3M launched a full line of privacy and antiglare films for laptops and PCs that leveraged the company's brand equity and sales presence in the office products market. Within five years the product line became one of 3M's biggest and fastest-growing businesses.

Assess and Contain Risk

The risk of disappointment pervades each stage of the innovation process. This is the reality of any pursuit of a new and untried match between a solution and a market need. Successful innovators confront these risks without blinking, and get them under control by making the underlying assumptions explicit and defensible, and taking actions that contain but do not avoid the risks. Their actions are initially guided by a rigorous screening using the Real-Win-Worth It framework. When the growth ini-tiative is fully realized, and reaches the decision to launch, the innovators use discovery-driven planning to challenge the business plan and the financial case for making an investment. They also adopt a real-options mode of thinking that seeks small initial investments and follows up on them depending on what is learned.

Challenge the Business Model

A diversified manufacturer became frustrated with the returns on its innovation investment. To get a better handle on the reasons, it assembled a database of the financial performance of major growth investments, and then persuaded some noncompeting firms to contribute their projects. The objective was to compare the projections of sales, share, and profitability used to justify and fund each project with the actual performance seven years from launch.

The results were startling. The profitability (ROI) *projections* (averaged across all the business plans in the study) presented an attractive long-run return—well above the cost of capital—and break-even returns within 20 months of commercialization. In *reality*, only 10% of all the projects beat the forecast. The median break-even was four and a half years, which would never have justified funding by corporate. The bottom 10% were still in the red after seven years.

I've shared these findings with many managers in many industries. Few are shocked. Most are not fazed even when it is pointed out that the study was limited to projects that were still in business after seven years. Many more certainly failed or were shut down during that time, and their performance would have made the picture even worse.

Most managers are sanguine about the absurdity of the early financial projections used to justify investment, and can readily explain the distortions. At the top of the list is *anchoring* on a target break-even or discounted cash flow ROI. It is easy to start with this target and adjust key cost, price, and adoption parameters to deliver the target result. The second culprit is *gamesmanship*. Resource allocation, too, is often seen as a zero-sum game, with "worthy" projects competing for the same scarce pool of investment dollars. If no advocate for a competing project presents less attractive forecasts, these worthy projects risk being pushed down the list of candidates. Since most managers are convinced their project is as good as the others, they rally a set of assumptions to support their case. Many other biases come into play. My favorite is the *confirmation bias*, in which we are all prone to select and embrace information that supports our beliefs and assumptions, and reject or ignore uncomfortable information that questions those assumptions. This is exacerbated by *overconfidence*, which makes us far too certain that our current assumptions are correct. Finally, development teams are prone to *groupthink*, in which all the members in a group learn to see the world the same way.

Firms that are confident in their ability to innovate recognize these ingrained biases and deal with them in several ways. First, they are unflinching in their postmortems of failures and disappointments,, and look for patterns in their assumptions that went consistently awry. Almost always these can be traced to less controllable market factors such as rate of market adoption, market share, or the trajectory of prices over time. Such postmortems are motivated by a desire to learn, not a thinly disguised search for someone to blame. The lessons are codified and retained, and they add to the cumulative intelligence of the firm and increase the odds that a stalled or failed project can be eventually repurposed.

Confident innovators know that informed and credible "outsiders" can usefully challenge the assumptions of a team that is passionate about bringing its project to market and likely to be dismissive about uncomfortable aspects. These external resource people may be successful innovators from other parts of the company or consultants who have deep experience in similar situations. Confident innovators focus on the underlying fundamentals that create cash flow and economic value; without sound assumptions underlying the projections of sales, costs, and profit returns, the financials don't deserve much weight. Finally, as part of their embrace of best practices, confident innovators use R-W-W screening to surface the critical assumptions at the genesis of the project. But as development and refinement proceeds to the point where serious money has to be committed, they will then turn to a valuable tool for deep discovery developed by Rita McGrath and Ian MacMillan: *discovery-driven planning*.[40] The logic of this approach, McGrath and MacMillan say, is "that as your plan unfolds, you want to be reducing what we call the assumption-to-knowledge ratio. When [this] ratio is high, there is a huge amount of uncertainty, and one should prioritize learning fast, at the lowest possible cost." As the ratio shrinks, focus and resource prioritization became more important.

To focus project teams on what truly matters, discovery-driven planning asks them first to list all the assumptions built into the initial projections. Then the critical question is "Which assumptions must prove true to ensure the projections can be realized?" Those assumptions are then classified by strategic importance and confidence. Scott Anthony has a nice way of prioritizing assumptions along these two dimensions. The matrix in Figure 3-3 shows at a glance which assumptions need to be validated and which can be taken as given.

Here are some potentially dangerous assumptions that should be challenged and validated:

- Customers will buy our product because it is technically superior.
- Distributors are willing to stock and service the product.

Figure 3-3
Prioritizing Assumptions

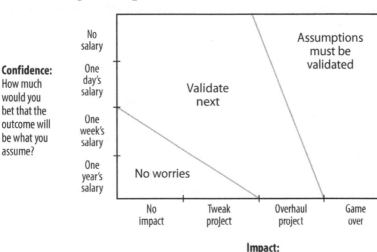

Impact:
What happens to your strategy if you are wrong?

- We can complete development on time and within budget.
- Competitors will respond rationally.
- Key influential and opinion leaders in this market will support us.
- The rest of the organization will willingly support our launch program.

In the panoply of dubious assumptions, these few are more dangerous than those behind the business plan for the Segway scooter.[41] This was an ingenious two-wheeled, battery-powered single-person transporter. It was launched at a price of $5,000, in order to cover the cost of a sophisticated dynamic-stabilization technology. The business plan called for sales to reach 40,000 scooters a month by the end of the first year.

Fast-forward five years: Only 23,000 scooters had been sold (a sales level closer to 400 per month). So, what went wrong? The assumed potential market for transportation over ranges of several miles in pedestrian-friendly environments such as sidewalks and airports was much smaller than expected. Only a few people had a strong, recurring need that was not already being met by walking or bicycling. For those with this need, a cheaper and simpler stand-up platform, one that added a small third wheel for stability, was sufficient.

Discovery-driven planning helps development teams and executives with resource-allocating authority to surface and challenge the potentially dangerous assumptions in the business plan. This approach to planning is based on a *reverse income statement*. As the label implies, the starting point is the desired operating profit. You then work backward to specify what must be accomplished to deliver that profit. Assumptions have to be surfaced about how much revenue is needed given the target return on sales; the costs to be incurred at each stage of the value chain to make, sell, and distribute the innovation; and the assets the project can support to realize the target ROI. Each of these estimates requires an explicit assumption, which is duly noted as part of the deliverables specification, covering all things that have to be done for the project to be successful. In the early stages of the project, where R-W-W is the tool of choice for surfacing those assumptions, there is a high likelihood they will go wrong. By the time the project is close to a decision to launch, a lot of learning has been done to squeeze out the uncertainty in the assumptions and fill out the reverse income statement with some measure of confidence.

Keep Your Options Open

When a business considers investing in a small-*i* innovation, close to their core they have a wealth of data to plug into the familiar net-present-value (NPV) and other discounted cash flow financial models. Out comes a (seemingly) rigorous answer to the question "Will the anticipated NPV return on investment in this project exceed our cost of capital?" Of course, all the cost, revenue, and other estimates are just that—assumptions that can be manipulated. However, an experienced senior manager who is familiar with the market, the competitors, and so on will readily detect any blatant exaggerations.

The financial analysis of adjacencies and BIG(ger)-*I* growth opportunities is far more problematic because there is so much uncertainty to be resolved. NPV approaches can actually impede strategic thinking. Instead what is needed is a wholly different approach to resource-allocation decisions, captured in the mantra "Think big...Start small...Fail cheap...Scale fast." More formally, what is needed is a real-options approach.[42]

A real option is a relatively small investment that creates the right, but not the obligation, to make further investments as the future unfolds. For this approach to work there has to be asymmetry in the distribution of returns, with greater upside potential than downside exposure to failure and loss. This happens when you can terminate the investment or otherwise contain any negative outcomes while retaining the right to make further investments if the initial foray seems promising. Your next step depends entirely on what you learn.

By keeping your options open, you are focusing more on cutting the cost of an early failure versus trying to reduce the rate of failure. You have to be willing to shut the option down but always stay open to learning from any disappointments to inform another new growth initiative. Best-practice companies have long adopted and benefited from this approach, and embrace the following activities:

- Rapid prototyping of preliminary designs or mock-ups, with concept tests or Internet test market studies to get rapid feedback on different variations.
- Creation of small-scale pilot to prove the production process or system, before scaling up at great expense before a full-scale launch.
- Toehold investments in small technology start-ups, with an option to buy a larger stake later. In the meantime you have a window into the prospects and pitfalls of an emerging technology.
- Outsourcing of some development and delivery elements of the initiative to specialized partners in the early stages, to keep risk exposure to a minimum. If the opportunity takes

off, you can commit to the next level of investment; if not, your loss is contained.

Real-options thinking also means accounting for follow-on growth opportunities that would not be accessible unless you launched the new initiative. These are often valued at zero, because they may not be realized. In my view this is dangerous, because it disadvantages the growth initiative. A healthier approach is to run a realistic NPV for the new venture, and if it falls short of some (risk-adjusted) threshold rate of return, you ask how much future cash flow would have to be realized from the exercise of growth options for the investment to be attractive. For example, Xiameter, the Web-enabled distribution platform for silicones developed by Dow Corning to compete in the price-sensitive market segment (and described more fully in the previous chapter) was apparently a marginally attractive investment if it was limited to silicones. What tipped the balance in favor of Xiameter was the explicit recognition that it was a robust and scalable platform for distributing any undifferentiated chemical compound such as ethylene glycol. This is just what happened, and because the fixed costs were already absorbed, the additional business from noncompeting companies was extremely profitable.

Develop and Launch the Best Opportunties

The payoff from a disciplined strategic growth process is the successful commercialization of a growth opportunity that really moves the growth dial. The final stage in this growth process is an embedded set of development processes designated to take the best opportunities speedily to market.

The purpose of the three filters featured in this chapter is to ensure convergence on attractive opportunities that can justify investment of scarce development talent and financial resources. The roles of each of these filters is shown stylistically in Figure 3-4, which features the number of new product concepts needed to successfully launch a single new product.[43] This schematic is limited by the original research, which dealt only with new products (and not the full spectrum of growth concepts), and does not distinguish small-*i* from BIG-*I* innovations. While dated, it gives a flavor of the rapid attrition of growth ideas during the convergence and development phases of the strategy process. The data are broadly consistent with our findings that 60–65% of all innovations are successful.

Figure 3-4
The Attrition Curve for Innovation Concepts

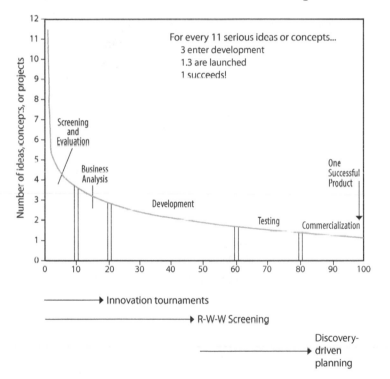

A noteworthy feature of this attrition curve is that 80% of the total time needed to bring a growth concept to market is consumed in the development, testing, and commercialization stages. This is why most of the literature in innovation emphasizes these activities. Our interest is in the broader strategic context for these project-specific activities.

Guidance for Managers: Examine Your Current Practices

I've never met a management team that has complained about a lack of opportunities. But they usually lack confidence that they have identified the best set of opportunities or that they can pick the best ones from a set of possibilities. To find where improvements are needed, I have found the following questions useful for interrogating the current practice and identifying areas for improvement:

- How are growth opportunities generated and then selected in response to a strategic challenge? Does the process engage a broad and informed slice of the organization? Are the most innovative thinkers tapped for their ideas?
- How is screening viewed by project teams and advocates of opportunities: as a go/no-go gate or as an opportunity to learn how to improve the growth initiative?
- How much time is spent on screening projects at various stages of development? How is this time viewed? As a distraction from the real work of innovation or as an opportunity to improve the project and get buy-in across the organization?
- Does your organization routinely undertake postmortems on failures/disappointments to diagnose the causes and identify places to make changes? How widely shared are these insights?
- Does your resource-allocation process rely mainly on financial projections to choose projects to fund? Are the underlying assumptions identified and validated?
- What financial measures are used to decide whether to fund a major investment in a growth initiative? Do these measures rely on familiar NPV approaches or consider real-options value?
- What kinds of real options has your company adopted in the past? Which have been the most and the least successful?

Chapter 4

Apply Innovation Prowess to Accelerate Growth

The 3M Company has long been recognized as a bastion of innovation prowess, and continually outperforms other diversified industrials.[44] At the heart is a culture that believes in customer-inspired innovation and an organization designed to listen to customers and act on their feedback. As Fred Palensky, 3M's chief technology officer explains, the company's outside-in approach is to "connect with the customers, find out their articulated and unarticulated needs, and then determine the capability at 3M that...could solve the customer's problem in a unique, proprietary and sustainable way." Its ability to find these solutions across the diversity of divisions depends on a culture of interdependence and sharing. While 3M is well known for providing time for engineers to pursue new ideas and experiment, the culture of idea sharing and joint learning is just as important. The company also converts a high volume of ideas into growth initiatives by providing multiple sources of funding, such as Genesis grants to fund experiments. Once an experiment looks promising, there are corporate resources to support their commercialization. Fear of failure is not a factor; the culture rewards "well intentioned failures" that offer useful lessons that can be repurposed and reused elsewhere.

The innovation prowess of growth leaders such as 3M, Diageo, Celgene, and LEGO enables them to see opportunities sooner, bring more and better initiatives successfully to market, improve innovation productivity by carefully containing the inevitable risks, and then gain advantages that are hard to match. Innovation prowess functions like organizational musculature, mobilizing and focusing these companies resources and realizing their strategic intentions.

Innovation prowess requires not just the process steps we've discussed in the prior chapters. The poet W. H. Auden once suggested that human beings never become something without pretending to be it first. Designing a disciplined growth-seeking process is in many ways "pretending" to have innovation prowess. It is a necessary first step. But innovation prowess is more than just the strategy process. If you don't address the people and organizational side of the equation, you will never be anything other than a pretender to growth leadership. Innovation prowess also requires the orchestration of three entwined organizational elements of innovation ability,[45] illustrated in Figure 4-1.

- **Culture.** An organization's shared values and beliefs, defining appropriate and inappropriate behaviors. It is often summed up simply as "the way we do things around here."
- **Capabilities.** The combination of skills, technology, and knowledge that allows the firm to execute specific activities and innovation processes. Not to be confused with assets, capabilities are the results of people and the tools available to them. A capability grows as it is exercised.
- **Configuration.** The structure of the organization, including how resources are allocated, who bears responsibility for achieving targets, and how success is measured. This is far more than an organizational chart—it is the dynamic flow of decisions and resources within the firm.

These elements are mutually reinforcing. They don't simply add together; instead they are multiplicative, as a weakness in one afflicts the others. An organization configured with rigid fiefdoms that protect their turf will subvert the sharing of market knowledge and undermine efforts to open up the culture. A culture that does not value customer feedback will not maintain the capabilities necessary to hear and integrate that feedback. Each of these elements is crucial, but culture matters most.

Efforts to build new innovation capabilities or improve the firm's configuration will succeed when they are supported by the appropriate cultural attributes. Conversely, a dysfunctional

Figure 4-1
Diagnosing an Innovation Ability

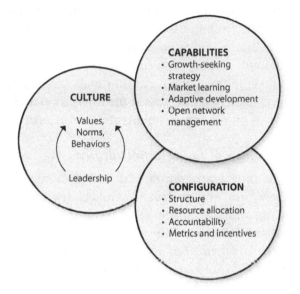

culture is hard to surmount. The poster child is Sony, who missed both the iPod (despite the lead in portable music the company gained with the Walkman) and the smartphone revolution. As Howard Stringer, the current CEO of Sony, who was brought in as an outsider and charged with changing the company's culture, wryly noted, "Love affairs with status quo continue even after the quo has lost its status."

That said, cultures cannot be created by fiat. They cannot be talked into existence even by the most charismatic leaders. Cultures evolve over time based on the behaviors modeled and encouraged by executives and reinforced by the firm's incentive structures. Because cultures are resistant to change in the short term, I'll focus here on driving cultural change via investing in capabilities and changes in configuration that encourage changes in behavior, which over time become embedded in the firm's culture. Before getting to that, however, it is useful to describe the goal: an innovation culture.

Innovation Culture

A culture has many levels and facets. At the deepest level are the traits or values that express enduring preferences or aspirations. The more accessible expression of these values are norms, which are shared beliefs about appropriate or expected *behavior*. The most obvious outcroppings of a culture are the behaviors that top managers and employees exhibit as they make choices about how to spend their time. Here the tone at the top is what matters most, so we will focus on the commitments and priorities of leadership.

Values and Norms of Innovation Cultures

There are no innovative organizations with shallow or forgettable cultures; there is no end of slogans extolling the special traits of innovative organizations. Innovation gurus urge firms to "share to gain," "always look for a win-win," "fail fast," and "learn from failures." Each has merit. But all reflect an all-too-common faith in "best practices." Innovation leaders don't follow best practices; instead they create new practices in response to deep questioning about what has to be done to raise their firm's performance to the next level.

Eventually these next practices are captured and explained in articles and books. But they are often distilled through a mix of conventional wisdom, with much of the context that made them useful stripped away. When A. G. Lafley became CEO of Procter & Gamble he faced a demoralized organization where the pace of innovation had declined dramatically. To center the organization, he adopted the mantra "Consumer is boss." The aim was to inculcate the notion that people who buy and use P&G products are valued not just for their money but also as a rich source of ideas and insights. With intense repetition and personal commitment, Lafley was able to embed this into the cultural values of the company.[46] His approach worked, but there is no reason necessarily to believe that the same mantra, especially if stripped of the context of Lafley's intense commitment to action rather than just sloganeering, would be successful elsewhere.

A recent study by Booz & Company[47] enumerated the cultural traits judged to be most important in a survey of senior officers:

1. Strong identification with the customers and an overall orientation toward customers (importance score = 0.62).
2. Passion for and pride in the products and services offered (0.50).
3. Reverence and respect for technical talent and knowledge (0.24).
4. Openness to new ideas from customers, suppliers, and competitors and other industries (0.23).
5. Culture of collaboration across functions and geographies (0.2).

It's at least mildly ironic that a study designed to capture and share new ideas found that the cultural value of being open to new ideas was scored so low. The importance of some of these attributes is supported by rigorous research—notably the vast body of studies on the positive effect of market orientation on innovativeness,[48] which in turn is highly correlated with financial performance. But in general the advice to be gleaned from such best-practice research falls into the "Mom and Apple Pie" category: ideas that everyone knows are good and few would disagree with. But such anodyne ideas don't propel an innovative culture.

In my experience, one of the key cultural commonalities among innovative organizations is the belief that more can be learned from the careful dissection of failures than from successes; a failure presents an opportunity to uncover and eliminate the mistake and build something better. Three other highly interrelated cultural traits seem to distinguish firms with innovation prowess.[49]

First, these firms are willing to cannibalize their own successful products. This requires an outside-in perspective that recognizes that customers will migrate to a better solution when it emerges, regardless of who provides it. Innovators would rather cannibalize themselves now than starve when customers move to the competitor who provides that better solution.

Second, there is a different attitude toward risk. These firms are willing to embrace the very high risk of innovation failure to escape the even higher risk of competitive defeat if they stand still. The likelihood of failure for any innovation initiative, especially beyond the firm's current capabilities, is dauntingly high, so there is a great temptation to keep investing in the core business because the risk-adjusted returns seem so appealing. But those returns are increasingly temporary and short term for firms unwilling to pursue the full spectrum of innovation possibilities.

The third key trait is a focus on the future. Innovative cultures downplay past and present successes, choosing to devote their energy to pursuing the next success. For instance, part of Toyota's culture is conducting a postmortem on *successful* projects to uncover opportunities for future improvement.

Leadership and Culture

The fingerprints of the leaders are imprinted on every aspect of a culture. The tone is set by the top person but is magnified by the rest of the C-Suite. When the leader is the founder, of course, it is his or her vision, priorities, and strength of character that have the greatest influence. Leaders populate the organization with people who respect the leader's values and exhibit patterns of behavior the leaders are comfortable with. Leaders who value innovation encourage people to take risks in pursuit of new ideas and opportunities. This gives everyone the courage to take risks because they are confident that the rest of the organization will stand behind them. In contrast, operational leaders with a short-term orientation tend to hire people who are cautious, creating a climate where failure leads to a search for someone to blame—with a chilling effect on innovation.

Jeff Bezos has shaped a robust culture of innovation at Amazon. In a recent interview[50] he explained how he selects people who are naturally innovative. He sends a powerful signal when he asks all job candidates, "Tell me about something you have invented." Innovation is both expected and valued. He especially looks for people who approach innovation from the outside in, and encourages improvements in customer experience by nurturing lots of experiments. Further, he feels that most of Amazon's biggest misses came from acts of omission rather than of commission. So he encourages his people to ask "Why not?" when considering whether to launch something new.

Leaders have many ways to shape the culture. One is how they spend their time; the more they devote to reviewing projects, working with teams, and recruiting talent, the faster their decision making. By understanding the project better, they can identify weak signals and inflection points the project team might miss. Many companies have regularly scheduled progress review meetings—as though innovation could be scheduled. Frequent interaction outside regular meetings can speed the interactive development activity that typifies innovation initiatives, and certainly it helps leadership to ask better questions.

Most new or rapidly growing firms have, somewhat taut-ologically, a culture that is innovation friendly. But as growth moderates—as it inevitably will—the firm's leadership faces a huge cultural challenge: Will the firm continue to pursue innovation even though there is now much more to lose? Will the firm transition to a more cautious stance? Will it emphasize extracting maximum value from its existing market position or maintain an outside-in focus, looking to what new markets and opportunities can be seized? A leader with an inside-out focus is likely to drift toward M&A opportunities rather than organic growth into adjacencies and beyond. As more investment and leadership attention is focused on transactions, the rest of the firm gets the message and the culture begins to change.

Typically, however, even leaders who want to nurture an innovation culture face a significant challenge. A period of rapid growth tends to weaken culture (as hiring outpaces the ability to "indoctrinate" new hires into the firm's cultural norms and beliefs) and outstrip existing organizational configurations and capabilities. The outside context is constantly changing as well. What worked in the past both internally and externally is unlikely to continue to work. Thus maintaining an innovation culture requires leaders willing to revisit the capabilities and configuration of the firm regularly to ensure they are furthering the firm's innovation prowess, deepening the innovation culture, and delivering organic growth.

Innovation Capabilities

Culture underlies and infuses everything an organization does. Capabilities are the sum of the skills and experience the firm collectively brings to the actions it takes. Culture and capabilities have a symbiotic relationship—one can't function without the other. They also have to be closely aligned to get superior results.

Capabilities are bundles of closely integrated skills, technologies, and cumulative learning—exercised through organizational processes. Every business acquires many capabilities to enable it to carry out the many activities needed to move its products and services through the value chain. Capabilities should not be confused with assets, which are the resources a business has accumulated. Investments in plants, patents, or systems are not capabilities because these are *things*, not skills. Capabilities are the glue that brings these assets together and enables them to be deployed advantageously. Capabilities also don't wear out over time; indeed, the more a capability is used, the better it becomes, because it incorporates more learning.

Four capabilities are needed to ensure a firm has a superior innovation prowess, meaning it can execute the underlying innovation processes better than its rivals. First and foremost is the capability to execute the disciplined strategy process that provides the organizing framework for the growth-seeking activities of the business and is the focus of this book. Supporting this strategy process is the *market learning capability*, which is integral to an outside-in approach. Third is the *open network management capability* that has reshaped innovation over the past two decades. Finally, there is the *adaptive development capability* for bringing the chosen growth initiative through development and testing to commercialization. Let's look at these three supporting capabilities more closely.

Market Learning Capability[51]

Useful insights into market opportunities and reactions to innovations don't emerge easily. Instead, insights must be actively sought, shared, and acted on via market sensing, sense making, applying insights, and learning from feedback. Keep in mind that all capabilities are driven by learning, where continuous exercise builds new layers of insight.

Market Sensing

This activity may be triggered by an impending decision or strategy review, an emerging problem, or a belief that an innovation initiative requires deeper insights into customer needs. This spark begins the active search and acquisition phase to acquire relevant and actionable information—including what is already stored in a firm's knowledge system and what managers throughout the company know. When this is done well, the company has the information it needs to anticipate where its markets are going, and to get there before its competitors.

Sense Making

For findings to be useful, they must be distilled so that coherent patterns can be recognized and converted into usable insights. Many errors are made during this stage, as managers misinterpret what they see in favor of what they want to see. Worse, they may dismiss results that don't conform to their expectations. For instance, insights are often lost or rejected when they challenge the prevailing wisdom. When one detergent maker decided to look for growth among noncommitted users, it formed a diverse team to study these users (mostly women). The aim was to understand the pressures of their lives, their needs and wants, and their feeling about their clothes. From these deep observations, the team came up with a new way to appeal to these customers' feminine sensibility. This ran counter to the senior managers' beliefs about how the brand should be positioned. To overcome these beliefs, the team dramatized its findings in a one-hour "play," with scripts derived from the verbatim recordings of the consumer immersion sessions.

Applying the Insights

This can happen close to the time when the insights are found, or much later if the firm has to dip into its knowledge stores to act on newly emerging opportunities. The longer the lag, the harder the firm needs to work to ensure the retrieval and application of old knowledge to new problems. Applying insights can be very fruitful for firms with a vast number of patents, for example. Considering an existing patent in light of emerging science, policies, or customer preferences can often generate new products. For example, Cognis, a large chemical manufacturer, developed a plant-based fabric softener—most softeners are based on animal fats—but it did not work well in water and hence could not be used effectively in washing machines. However, while working with a developer of moist dryer sheets, Cognis saw the opportunity to apply its existing technology. In partnership with Arm & Hammer, it launched Total 2-in-1 Dryer Cloths—a liquid fabric softener and an antistatic agent in one dryer sheet.

Feedback and Deeper Learning

Firms with a strong market learning capability actively seek and integrate lessons from what actually happened into their innovation activities and processes. Did the market respond as expected, and if not, why not? How could the process and the methodologies be improved? When widely disseminated through the firm, these lessons continue to improve practice. This is much more likely to happen when the culture is supportive and treats failures as disappointments with rich learning opportunities.

Open Network Management Capability

The term *open* is rich in positive connotations, including expansiveness, flexibility, sharing, and ready access. It is increasingly applied to innovation processes as a consequence of (1) advances in communication networks and deeper understanding of how to coordinate diverse players with different interests, (2) the recognition by many firms "that not all the smart people in the industry work for us"; and (3) celebrated success stories such as Procter & Gamble's Connect + Develop innovation model.[52]

There is a wide variety of open innovation networks. Here is a sampling:

- **Co-development, by working with outside partners.** These projects can evolve to a joint venture or alliance in which the partners enter a formal, legal sharing arrangement in the form of a new entity.
- **Innovation brokers such as InnoCentive and NineSigma, which help firms search for ideas and help inventors find markets for their ideas.** A firm will work with a broker to solve a specific problem, from imagining a new feature to creating a new polymer with specific properties, by posing the problem to a selected global community.
- **Customer co-creation.** This puts customers at the center of the innovation process. Think about stuffed toys, where innovation traditionally has meant anticipating demand for a new design and manufacturing it to get it on the shelves. In a complete departure from this approach, the Build-a-Bear Workshop creates a platform to help customers design their own stuffed animals. Children buy an empty shell of an animal and then give it an identity with personalized sounds, clothing, and accessories. The result is an engaging customer experience.
- **Employee social networks.** Yum! Brands (parent of A&W, Taco Bell, KFC, and Pizza Hut) offers its 300,000 employees an internal social network and collaboration tool, and encourages them to use it regularly to solve problems and share best practices.

When an open innovation network is under the control of the focal firm, it operates more like a private club. Here, you tackle an opportunity with one or more collaborators you select because they have the necessary resources without unmanageable conflicts of interest. This kind of structure is well suited to innovating complex solutions that solve customer problems. For example, Janssen (Pharmaceuticals) helps doctors overcome the problem of schizophrenia patients missing their medications (which is an issue for about 30% of patients at any given time). Working with payers, doctors, nurses, schedulers, clinics, and a host of implementation partners, Janssen managed all the steps in the distribution of a drug to an injection site to overcome the barriers for patients.

The interwoven nature of open innovation networks is revealed in the portrayal of some possible partner combinations in Figure 4-2. Although this "ball of yarn" schematic may seem dauntingly complex, some firms have developed the capability to effectively manage the linkages for mutual benefit. This requires a new suite of skills and experience that is difficult to learn but also difficult to copy, making the investment in developing this capability likely to pay off handsomely. The benefits of accelerated innovation development, a richer array of possible solutions, and more ways of sharing risk with partners make the effort worthwhile. But what skills and knowledge are needed?

Mapping and Engaging the Ecosystem

The skills and activities here begin with learning about possible partners, inside and outside the firm, who can contribute to a particular innovation effort. A good way to capture this learning is by creating a map of possible partners. Once partners have been identified it is useful to pool knowledge and seek the maximum number of connections to external partners—these connections are often helpful for ensuring that selected partners will readily integrate into the innovation effort. Many General Electric businesses have participated in network "Action Workouts." The aim is to bring together all the implementers inside the business to identify and map their ecosystem, plus all the possible players outside GE who would need to innovate and agree to adopt in order for the project to succeed.

Figure 4-2
Innovating in an Open Network

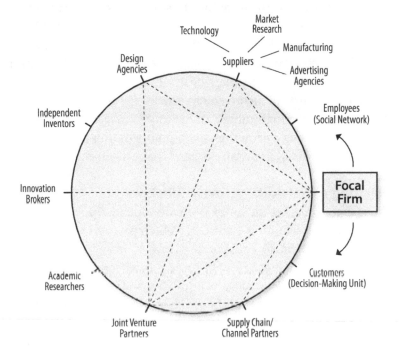

Identify and Contain Risks

Open innovation networks bring a whole set of new and different risks to identify and contain. Probing the roles and linkages in the map of the ecosystem exposes two kinds of risk—each requiring a specific action plan: (1) co-innovation risk, stemming from your dependence on others to innovate in parallel; and (2) adoption chain risk, which is the extent to which partners will need to adopt your innovation before consumers can actually assess the full value proposition.[53]

When introduced in September 2006, Sony's eReader was initially hailed as the iPod of the book industry. However, Sony's failure to identify and contain the risks of launching an innovation dependent for success on other participants in the market means the device barely has 10% of the global market. As a device, the Sony eReader was exceptional: slim, lightweight, and easy to navigate, with the ability to search, find, and store many books. Yet a great device is of little value without accessible and desirable content. This was the Sony eReader's Achilles' heel. As Ron Adner observes, "It was easier to head to the local bookstore or order a book online than deal with a spotty inventory, an arbitrary backlist, an inconvenient process for getting e-books into the eReader, and high prices." Had Sony management had a true outside-in perspective on these pain points (rather than an inside-out hardware fixation), it would surely have taken a different path.

Relating to Network Partners/Collaborators

Bringing to market an innovation developed through an open network poses daunting questions: Which partners to select? How to motivate them to collaborate? How to keep them happy as circumstances change? How to protect intellectual property, and ensure that economic value is equitably shared? The answers to these questions are beyond the scope of this book, but fortunately the literature on alliances, joint ventures, and cross-licensing[54] offers clear guidance on the systems, people, and structural mechanisms for managing and coordinating partners.

Adaptive Development Capability

Most firms use some form of a phase-gate or stage-gate development[55] process to bring their innovation concepts to market. This process breaks the development process into a natural sequence of steps needed to move a chosen concept to launch. Each stage begins with a gate or go/no-go decision point, when senior management reviews progress with the development teams and decides whether to proceed to the next stage. Thus there is a lot of attrition as each stage becomes another filter. This enables "pay-as-you-go" project funding, with resources available for the next step only when there is acceptable progress against project metrics such as schedule, development budget, prototype performance, and cost-to-build. This stage-gate has a seemingly tidy, linear, and sequential appearance, as befits its origin in NASA engineering projects. In reality, it is iterative, halting, messy, and time consuming.

There are striking differences among firms in their development capability. According to Arthur D. Little,[56] the top performing firms are five times as productive as the average. That is, they realize five times as much output in terms of new product revenues or profits, for the same investment in R&D and new product development costs and time.

The most capable firms have improved their development processes in many ways. First, instead of a one-size-fits-all stage-gate template, there will be heavyweight and lightweight versions for small-*i* adjacency and BIG-*I* projects (see Figure 4-3). These variations in the development process account for the greater ambiguity of adjacencies and BIG-*I* innovations. An "efficient" standard approach[57] to each gate (appropriate for small-*i* projects) sets early targets, under the assumption that learning during later stages will reinforce and elaborate the early stages. This confers too much certainty to the process. In reality, as development of a BIG-*I* innovation proceeds, there will be surprises (both fortuitous and calamitous), and underlying assumptions will be articulated and challenged—requiring rethinking.

Further gains come from moving to "leaner" gates. Instead of the lengthy and time-consuming preparation of gate deliverables by the team, a brief document with a few backup slides is all that is expected. The gatekeepers are expected to arrive at the meeting already knowing the project, and are simply informed at the gate review about the risks and commitments to be made. Best-practice firms are simplifying their processes, and focusing more on the deliverables and clarity of responsibilities. Thus LEGO was able to cut average development time from 36 months in 1999 to 12 months in 2010,[58] with higher success rates. Standardized checklists were eliminated, and authority for deciding which activities were needed to demonstrate viability at each stage was delegated to the project teams.

Figure 4-3
Variations on Stage-Gate Processes

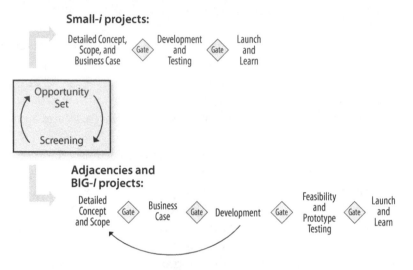

Innovation Configuration

A robust culture and well-honed innovation capabilities are not enough to ensure superior innovation prowess. The final ingredient is an organizational configuration that can align all the elements, allocate resources effectively, allow people to perform to their potential, and assign responsibility for achieving the results. A configuration is not complete until the entire C-Suite concurs wholeheartedly with answers to the following questions:

- Who is accountable at the highest level for reaching the growth objective? What happens when the growth objective is missed?
- How are resources (people, investment capital, and annual budgets) allocated? What happens when resources are trapped in the core?
- How do you keep score? What are the key metrics in the innovation dashboard? What incentive is there for individuals and teams to meet the targets on these metrics?
- Who is responsible for identifying, selecting, and training people, and then assigning them to teams?

These organizational questions cannot be avoided. The best answers to them will emerge from a process of introspection about what has worked in the past plus insights from other firms, and an honest confrontation of the organizational inhibitors to growth. There is no set formula; instead, the configuration will be shaped by legacy factors, competitive and market realities, and the determination of leadership to improve. However the answers emerge, the two most effective levers for the leaders to pull, in my experience, are the structural design and the choice of metrics and incentives.

Designing the Organization to Innovate

Rethinking an organizational structure is not like zero-based budgeting or starting with a blank sheet of paper. Instead, there is a history of hits and misses to learn from and inspire improvement. This requires everyone to agree on the persistent inhibitors to growth that are holding the organization back, and the changes needed to overcome these drags on performance. There are three structural inhibitors to growth that need to be overturned:[59]

Growth Inhibitor One: Diffused Accountability

You are likely a victim of this inhibitor if you are congenitally late to market with the small innovations needed to stay ahead of competition and to adapt to new customer requirements in the core business. A frequent structural reason is unclear accountability for results, which is exacerbated by shifting priorities and too many projects competing for the same resources. The problem may lie with IT, manufacturing, or the supply chain, but the "lightweight" project manager who is normally responsible for bringing all the functional disciplines together is either not the right person or lacks influence because he or she lacks budget authority.

Careful diagnosis of this inhibitor will reveal whether it can be abated with proper oversight by a working committee of senior people using aggressive portfolio reviews, and by assignment of small cross-functional teams to priority projects. Although there may be fewer projects at any given time, each is completed faster, and the result is more projects completed.

Growth Inhibitor Two: Constrained Thinking/Narrowed Thinking

When this inhibitor is at work, the spectrum of opportunities sought or pursued is too narrow and breakaway business model innovations are hard to design and nurture. When General Electric began accelerating its growth engine across its 14 business units in 2006, it recognized that reaching its stretch goals for organic growth required more than the traditional emphasis on applying new technology to global markets. To bring a more outside-in perspective and widen the spectrum of opportunities for growth, the company instituted a disciplined strategic growth process. This was led by the corporate chief marketing officer, Beth Comstock. In turn, she worked with business unit leaders to install qualified marketers within the leadership team of each business unit, to take the lead role in the growth agenda. These moves were supported and endorsed by the personal commitment of the CEO, Jeffrey Immelt, and embedded by first diversifying the top ranks (and reducing mobility so the business leaders were in place long enough to reap the rewards of their growth initiatives), investing in training and capability building, and tying incentives to innovation metrics.

Growth Inhibitor Three: Square Peg, Round Hole

Force-fitting BIG(ger)-*I* initiatives into the existing organization can be a major growth inhibitor. Cargill Corp. has grown and prospered as a large-scale player in the global agriculture and food-supply chain. In common with many large, mature companies, it felt it was not fully exploiting opportunities that didn't fit comfortably within an existing business unit. Existing incentives in the firm actually discouraged the managers of businesses from taking bigger and longer-term risks, even with the promise of high returns. For example, the Cargill division selling standard ice-melting chemicals to state road departments had mastered a low-cost supply chain. This was not a supportive setting for a novel de-icing chemical—an epoxy overlay that inhibited the formation of ice—sold for critical applications such as bridges and freeway ramps. The business model didn't fit the existing structure, and required new skills to make a sale.

Many organization models have been proposed for overcoming the problem of a square peg in a round organizational hole. Cargill successfully created a full-service group called the Emerging Business Accelerator, to shepherd attractive opportunities from outside the core by staffing, funding, and monitoring those opportunities until they could be spun out or folded back into an established Cargill business. This is an example of what Wolcott and Lippitz[60] designate as "focused organizational ownership" and "dedicated resource authority." There are many variants, depending on whether organizational ownership is diffused and opportunities bubble up within the operating businesses, or resources are dispersed in an ad hoc fashion, or there is a dedicated budget or strategic reserve for noncore opportunities. The key is to make sure opportunities are not smothered or starved of resources by being forced to fit uncomfortably within an existing operating unit.

Metrics and Incentives

A dashboard of innovation metrics has many uses. It is essential for identifying the weak links in the overall innovation process, as well as costly disconnects between the growth strategy and the portfolio of growth initiatives. It is also needed to hold mangers accountable, by setting targets for improvement and linking incentives to target achievement. An adroitly chosen metric with a challenging target is a strong signal of a shift in strategic priorities. Part of A. G. Lafley's successful transformation of the innovation process at Procter & Gamble was setting a goal of acquiring 50% of P&G's innovations from outside the company.

A useful innovation dashboard should include measures of *inputs*, such as the number of concepts in the pipeline; *process measures*, such as average time to market; and *performance outcomes*, such as the percentage of sales from new products over several years, customer satisfaction, and the NPV of the portfolio. Yet most managers are unhappy with their dashboards.

There are two main reasons for this.[61] First, there is an emphasis on results over diagnostic insights. Five of the seven most popular metrics found in the survey measured either financial results or customer satisfaction. But suppose the results are poor? Most dashboards lack an ability to find the reason. Second, there is a lack of accountability for moving the innovation dial. Most companies are unable to directly connect either individual or group incentives to innovation activity, often because of the paucity of diagnostic/intermediate process improvement measures.

Designing a dashboard requires balancing identifying strategically insightful measures (rather than just those that are easy to collect) against collecting too many measures, and thereby diffusing focus. I offer two lessons based on my own and others' research.

Emphasize Learning over Scorekeeping

The weight of metrics should shift toward input and process effectiveness measures. But which are most useful? In my experience, few companies are short of ideas—the real problem is a lack of ideas that are worth pursuing. Insightful metrics will reveal loose screening that keeps too many poor ideas in the pipeline, sloppy processes causing delays in hitting the stage gates, or poor product quality that requires recycling the project back through development. Whirlpool, as an example, has a real-time dashboard so that any manager can see how many concepts are in process, which part of the globe they are coming from, and how many are headed for commercialization. Whirlpool executives pay close attention to these metrics, as roughly 30% of their compensation is tied to innovation performance.

Customize the Dashboard

One size does not fit all firms, and there are no "silver bullet" metrics. Instead, a useful innovation dashboard passes three tests: First, it reflects the strategic priorities and is customized for the market. (What is useful for a bioscience firm with lengthy development cycles won't apply to a packaged goods firm and vice versa.) Second, it gives a holistic picture of the entire innovation process. Third, it recognizes that all metrics are flawed and susceptible to gaming. Thus a good dashboard yields insights by a process of triangulation in which several metrics taken together yield a fuller picture.

Firms with innovation prowess use rigorous approaches to ask which metrics give the most useful insights, have a demonstrable impact on business results, can be influenced by management action, and will be trusted by the organization. The reality for Merck, as with all pharmaceutical companies, is that it needs to evaluate 10,000 new compounds a year, with 6 to 12 years per drug launch spent in development. Unsurprisingly, 92% of its development budget is spent on failures. Its most useful metrics are: time spent in each development phase compared with competition, mean time to failure, and the full economic value of the drug pipeline.

Henkel, the German packaged goods giant, sees a very different market reality. Many small new products are launched each year, failure rates after launch are very high, development times are short, and competitors match successful moves quickly. Henkel's choice of innovation metrics was strongly influenced by a study of 2,237 new products launched by Henkel and four competitors over three and half years. There were striking differences among companies in the returns from their new product efforts as revealed by measures of: new product share; relative number of launches (an indicator of activity but not necessarily of progress); launches that gained more than 1 percent share; and average brand share change, which showed whether new products were building or just replacing share for their existing products.

Improving and Applying Your Innovation Prowess

Our emphasis in this playbook for managers has been on the strategic front end of the innovation activities that drive superior organic growth. We believe that success is grounded in a disciplined and purposeful approach. This is both enabled and constrained by the innovation ability of the organization. Superior innovation ability requires the orchestration of a supportive culture, superior capabilities, and an appropriate configuration. The next step on the journey to accelerate the organic growth rate is an assessment of your ability, informed by the best practices and research in this chapter. In the following section, "Guidance for Managers," the questions can help provoke and guide a dialogue within the leadership team on how to introduce discipline and perseverance into the organic growth process. The rewards are worth the journey. Good luck!

Guidance for Managers: Assess Your Innovation Ability

There is no room for complacency within either growth leaders or growth laggards about their innovation ability. Growth leaders should be looking over their shoulder and constantly seeking improvements to stay ahead. Growth laggards need to dissect the three elements of their ability, to learn what is holding them back. Here are some suggestive questions to guide the search for improvement by both kinds of companies:

Our Culture?
- Does our culture expect and value innovation? What are the indicators? Who are the role models?
- Are we risk averse or risk embracing? How well do we cope with disappointments? Are these seen as learning opportunities?
- Does the emphasis on extracting returns from current operations suppress thinking about growth opportunities?
- Does our culture activity encourage the sharing of knowledge and best practices?
- How open are we to new ideas from outside our company?

- Who are the main listening posts from emerging customer requirements? Do we believe that real understanding about customers comes from living with them?
- Are we prepared to transform our business before we have to? Are we willing to cannibalize ourselves?

Our Capabilities?

- Is our process for setting a growth strategy disciplined (with replicable activities and balanced resource allocations) or ad hoc and reactive?
- Are we able to identify and pursue growth initiatives across the full spectrum of opportunities, or do certain pathways always take priority?
- Are we better or worse than others in our industry at understanding and anticipating customer needs?
- Do we have a systematic capability for continuous experimenting in our market and learning?
- Are we more or less supportive of external/partnering collaboration than our rivals? Are we considered a good company to partner with?
- How well equipped are we to map our ecosystem and identity and select the best partnering prospects? Do we know how best to motivate partners to collaborate?

Our Configuration?

- How well equipped are we to manage opportunities outside our core business? Are we organized differently for small-*i*, BIG-*I* and adjacency growth initiatives?
- How well communicated and understood is our growth strategy?
- Is there clear accountability for reaching the growth objective? How well equipped are we to assess the effectiveness of our innovation efforts?
- How are resources actually allocated? Are long-run investments in BIG-*I* initiatives adequately protected?

- Is there internal consistency between, on the one hand, our metrics, rewards, and incentives and, on the other, our top management priorities?
- How satisfied are we with our innovation dashboard? How well does it reflect our strategic priorities? Does it emphasize learning for scorekeeping?

Conclusion

Have you been provoked or challenged by one of the TED Talks, or presentations from Singularity University? The video *Did You Know?/Shift Happens* takes just four minutes to jolt you with facts and predictions like the following examples.

- China will soon become the number one English speaking country in the world.
- Today's learner will have 10 to 14 jobs before they are 38 years old.
- The top 10 jobs in demand in 2010 did not exist in 2004.
- There are 12 billion searches on Google each month.
- It took Google+ just a year to reach 50 million people—whereas radio took 38 years.
- The amount of new technology is doubling every two years.

This is a future of exponential change and turbulence. For growth leaders, this is an opportunity to stretch their lead. To capitalize on these opportunities, they will have to accelerate their innovation engine. This will require strategic discipline, an unrelenting outside-in focus on creating new value for customers, and the adroit management of uncertainty. The fuel for the engine is their innovation ability, achieved with a supportive and adaptive culture, and world-class capabilities, while making sure the organization itself doesn't get in the way. With their growth-seeking strategic discipline giving direction to this innovation ability, their innovation prowess will be hard to equal.

Past innovation success is no guarantee of future success, especially in turbulent times. Too often, success leads to over-confidence and complacency, which erode discipline and add rigidity that slows the response to opportunities. What happened to one-time powerhouses such as Sony and Sharp, or the photographic giant Kodak? They invested in small-*i* innovations but were slow to respond to BIG-*I* challenges. These days, global pharmaceutical giants are casting around for new growth paths as their drug development pipelines are constricting.

In a world of relentless change, intense global competition, and unstoppable innovation, how can growth laggards keep up or even catch up? Here are five sturdy handrails for managers that capture the key lessons of this book. Their guidance will help firms accelerate their organic growth rate.

Handrail 1: Focus Relentlessly on Customer Value

A true outside-in posture keeps a business ahead of market and technology changes. The growth leaders start with a profound sense of what is actually in the customer's interest. They are notable for an external, active, and inquisitive orientation; they listen to a wide array of sources and are willing to challenge the prevailing wisdom if it is out of step with emerging realities. Being truly outside in opens up a much wider spectrum of growth opportunities.

An unrelenting focus on customers does not mean employees are not equally important. The challenge for the senior managers is to have employees whose passions and priorities are aligned with those of their customers. But if the top team doesn't take care of its employees, it will not surface customer needs or keep solving customer problems. Every level and function of the organization has to have people who are living with customers, attuned to what they are experiencing, and empathizing with their frustrations and problems. This cannot be achieved if the top team is isolated from their market and doesn't make superior customer value its priority.

Handrail 2: Balance Discipline and Creativity

Growth leaders are disciplined, both in their replicable processes for identifying and exploiting opportunities and for maintaining a balanced allocation of resources across a portfolio of growth initiatives. They can balance long-run and immediate pressing needs, and provide a clear growth road map to the entire organization. This doesn't mean procedural rigidity, unproductive formality, and time-killing approvals.

There should be a healthy tension between the creative risk-taking and experimenting part of the innovation culture and the disciplined, rigorous, and results-oriented part: an innovative organization needs both right- and left-brain functions. If one dominates the other, performance will surely suffer. When divergent and creative thinking are celebrated by the culture, the ideas will flow but the development process will be clogged with too many projects competing for scarce resources. The management team has to tolerate and encourage "well-intentioned" failures that occur for unexpected and unplanned reasons, while extracting lessons to improve the process and the next round of innovations. Without such tolerance, the people working on individual projects will avoid risks. Then the culture will subvert the process, and all the outcome measures will suffer. Innovation discipline is susceptible to the law of "fast forgetting." Unless the top team stays vigilant, innovation activities become reactive in response to demands from customers and sales people to make small-*i* adjustments to meet competition or pressing requirements. The antidote to this is to ensure there is widespread involvement in the choice of growth strategy and goals, coupled with clear team accountability for reaching those goals.

Handrail 3: Profit from Uncertainty

Throughout this book we have confronted the inherent uncertainty shrouding the prospects for any innovation. There is the attraction of the upside opportunity for faster growth, which comes burdened with downside threats from technology, market, and competitive uncertainty. However, there is no reason to become paralyzed by uncertainty. Leave that to the competitors, who watch your moves and wonder why they are always trying to catch up. Growth laggards struggle because imitative and reactive responses seldom deliver superior customer value or adequate profit returns. Growth leaders stay ahead by nurturing a risk-tolerant culture that is ready to make moves that cannibalize the sales of established products and endorse continuous experimentation. (Recall the mantra of so many growth leaders: "Think big...Start small...Fail cheap...Scale fast.") They also master key tools such as scenario thinking, real-options thinking, and discovery-driven planning, for realistically assessing and containing risk.

Handrail 4: Master Ambidexterity

An ambidextrous person is equally adept with both hands, a fairly rare skill. An ambidextrous organization can simultaneously explore new opportunities while exploiting the current business for maximum short-run gain. This is also a rare skill, one that has been mastered by growth leaders and gives them a decided edge. What makes it challenging to copy is that it takes innovation prowess at three levels.

First, it means being able to *diverge* with a search for opportunities along a full spectrum of growth pathways, while exercising the discipline to *converge* in a few high-potential prospects with an attractive balance of risk and reward.

Second, balance the discipline to build a formal and well-argued growth plan based on rigorous analysis, with trial-and-error experimentation that tests frequently and learns quickly. Growth leaders are especially adroit at recognizing experiments that succeed while cutting their losses and avoiding blind alleys. They let their resources follow the best opportunities within the overall growth strategy.

Third, at the organization level, ambidexterity mandates putting BIG-*I* initiatives and even adjacencies into a separate part of the organization, reporting to the top team. Such a separation from the existing organization, with its tested processes, and shorter-term incentives and controls, is essential to giving them breathing room. You can't fit a square peg into a round hole without a lot of pain and disappointment.

Handrail 5: Mobilize the Entire Organization

Innovation is a team sport. But who is on the team? With the advent of open innovation, growth leaders are finding new answers. Their organization extends beyond their core, to embrace the insourcing of ideas and talent from the outside. This is not the same as outsourcing, where an innovation activity is turned over to an outside partner (although, this maybe a good idea). Instead, the "ready-to-go" idea or solution to a technical problem is found in the extended network outside the firm. The experience of Procter & Gamble and others is that such ideas are bigger and create more economic value.

Growth leaders never forget that their growth strategies must be sold—not just communicated—to every employee. When all the pieces of the growth strategy come together, every employee at every level can see how their ideas and activities can support growth, and they are motivated to take the initiative. By mobilizing everyone, the firm can confidently apply its innovation prowess to accelerate their rate of organic growth.

Appendix A: Positioning Projects on the Matrix

Position each innovation product or concept by completing each statement in the left-hand column with one of the options offered across the top to arrive at a score from 1 to 5. Add the six scores in the Intended Market section to determine the project's x-axis coordinate on the risk matrix. Add the second scores in the Product/Technology section to determine its y-axis coordinate.

Intended Market							
	Be the same as in our present market		Partially overlap with our present market		Be entirely different from our present market or are unknown		
Customers' behavior and decision-making processes will...	1	2		3	4	5	
Our distribution and sales activities will...	1	2		3	4	5	
The competitive set (incumbents or potential entrants) will...	1	2		3	4	5	
	Highly relevant		Somewhat relevant		Not at all relevant		
Our brand promise is...	1	2		3	4	5	
Our current customer relationships are...	1	2		3	4	5	
Our knowledge of competitors' behavior and intentions is...	1	2		3	4	5	
					Total		
					(x-axis coordinate)		

Product/Technology							
	Is fully applicable		Will require signficant adaptation		Is not applicable		
Our current development capability...	1	2		3	4	5	
Our technology competency...	1	2		3	4	5	
Our intellectual property protection...	1	2		3	4	5	
Our manufacturing and service delivery system...	1	2		3	4	5	
	Are identical to those of our current offerings		Overlap somewhat with those of our current offerings		Completely differ from those of our current offerings		
The required knowledge and science bases...	1	2		3	4	5	
The necessary product and service functions...	1	2		3	4	5	
The expected quality standards...	1	2		3	4	5	
					Total		
					(y-axis coordinate)		

Appendix B: The Real-Win-Worth It Screen

Figuring out whether a market exists and whether a product can be made to satisfy that market are the first steps to screening a product concept. Those steps will indicate the degree of opportunity for any firm considering the potential market, so the inquiring company can assess how competitive the environment might be right from the start.

One might think that asking if the envisioned product is even a possibility should come before investigating the potential market. But establishing that the market is real takes precedence for two reasons: First, the robustness of a market is almost always less certain than the technological ability to make something. This is one of the messages of the risk matrix, which shows that the probability of a product failure becomes greater when the *market* is unfamiliar to the company than when the *product or technology* is unfamiliar. Second, establishing the nature of the market can head off a costly "technology push." This syndrome often afflicts companies that emphasize how to solve a problem rather than what problem should be solved or what customer desires need to be satisfied.

Is the market real?

A market opportunity is real only when four conditions are satisfied: (1) the proposed product will clearly meet a need or solve a problem better than available alternatives; (2) customers are able to buy it; (3) the potential market is big enough to be worth pursuing; and (4) customers are willing to buy the product.

Is there a need or desire for the product? Unmet or poorly satisfied needs must be surfaced through market research using observational, ethnographic, and other tools to explore customers' behaviors, desires, motivations, and frustrations. Once a need has been identified, the next question is *Can the customer buy it?* Even if the proposed product would satisfy a need and offer superior value, the market isn't real when there are objective barriers to purchasing that product.

The team next needs to ask, *Is the size of the potential market adequate?* A market opportunity isn't real unless there are enough potential buyers to warrant developing the product.

Finally, the team must ask, *Will the customer buy the product?* Are there subjective barriers to purchasing it? If alternatives to the product exist, customers will evaluate them and consider, among other things, whether the new product delivers greater value in terms of features, capabilities, or cost.

Is the product real?

Once a company has established the reality of the market, it should look closely at the product concept and expand its examination of the intended market.

Is there a clear concept? Before development begins, the technology and performance requirements of the concept are usually poorly defined, and team members often have diverging ideas about the product's precise characteristics. This is the time to expose those ideas and identify exactly what is to be developed. As the project progresses and the team becomes immersed in market realities, the requirements should be clarified.

Can the product be made? If the concept is solid, the team must next explore whether a viable product is feasible. Could it be created with available technology and materials, or would it require a breakthrough of some sort? If the product can be made, can it be produced and delivered cost-effectively, or would it be so expensive that potential customers would shun it?

Will the final product satisfy the market? During development, trade-offs are made in performance attributes, unforeseen technical manufacturing or systems problems arise, and features are modified. At each such turn in the road, a product designed to meet customer expectations may lose some of its potential appeal. Failure to monitor these shifts can result in the launch of an offering that looked great on the drawing board but falls flat in the marketplace.

Can we win?

Simply finding a real opportunity doesn't guarantee success. The more real the opportunity, the more likely it is that hungry competitors are eyeing it, too. And if the market is already established, incumbents will defend their positions by copying or leapfrogging any innovations.

The questions at this stage of the R-W-W screening carefully distinguish between the offering's ability to succeed in the marketplace and the company's capacity—through resources and management talent—to help it do so.

Can the product be competitive? Customers will choose one product over alternatives if it's perceived as delivering superior value with some combination of benefits such as better features, lower life-cycle cost, and reduced risk. The team must assess all sources of perceived value for a given product and consider the question *Does it have a competitive advantage?* Can someone else's offering provide customers with the same results or benefits?

Can the advantage be sustained? The first line of defense is patents. The project team should evaluate the relevance of its existing patents to the product in development and decide what additional patents may be needed to protect related intellectual property. It should ask whether a competitor could reverse-engineer the product or otherwise circumvent patents that are essential to the product's success.

How will competitors respond? A good place to start is a "red team" exercise: If we were going to attack our own product, what vulnerabilities would we find? How can we reduce them? A common error companies make is to assume that competitors will stand still while the new entrant fine-tunes its product prior to launch. Thus the team must consider what competing products will look like when the offering is introduced, how competitors may react after the launch, and how the company could respond. Finally, the team should examine the possible effects of this competitive interplay on prices. Would the product survive a sustained price war?

Can our company be competitive? After establishing that the offering can win, the team must determine whether the company's resources, management, and market insight are better than those of the competition. If not, it may be impossible to sustain advantage, no matter how good the product.

Do we have superior resources? The odds of success increase markedly when a company has or can get resources that both enhance customers' perception of the new product's value and surpass those of competitors. Superior engineering, service delivery, logistics, or brand equity can give a new product an edge by better meeting customers' expectations.

Do we have appropriate management? Does the organization have direct or related experience with the market, are its development-process skills appropriate for the scale and complexity of the project, and does the project both fit company culture and have a suitable champion. Success requires a passionate cheerleader who will energize the team, sell the vision to senior management, and overcome skepticism or adversity along the way.

Can we understand and respond to the market? Successful product development requires a mastery of market research tools, openness to customer insights, and the ability to share those insights with development team members. Repeatedly seeking the feedback of potential customers to refine concepts, prototypes, and pricing ensures that products won't have to be recycled through the development process to fix deficiencies.

Is it worth doing?

Just because an opportunity can pass the tests up to this point doesn't mean it is worth pursuing.

Will the product be profitable at an acceptable risk? Few products launch unless top management is persuaded that the answer to the question *Are forecasted returns greater than costs?* is definitely yes. This requires projecting the timing and amount of capital outlays, marketing expenses, costs and margins; applying time to break-even, cash flow, NPV, and other standard financial performance measures; and estimating the profitability and cash flow from both aggressive and cautious launch plans. Financial projections should also include the cost of product extensions and enhancements needed to keep ahead of the competition.

Are risks acceptable? A forecast's riskiness can be initially assessed with a standard sensitivity test: How will small changes in price, market share, and launch timing affect cash flows and break-even points? A big change in financial results stemming from a small change in input assumptions indicates a high degree of risk. The financial analysis should consider opportunity costs: committing resources to one project may hamper the development of others.

Does launching the product make strategic sense? Even when a market and a concept are real, the product and the company could win, and the project could be profitable, it may not make strategic sense to launch. The first question to ask is *Does the product fit our overall growth strategy?* In other words, will it enhance the company's capabilities by, for example, driving the expansion of manufacturing, logistics, or other functions? Will it have a positive or a negative impact on brand equity? Will it cannibalize or improve sales of the company's existing products? (If the former, is it better to cannibalize one's own products than to lose sales to competitors?) Will it enhance or harm relationships with stakeholders-dealers, distributors, regulators, and so forth? Does the project create opportunities for follow-on business or new markets that would not be possible otherwise?

Notes

1 Joanna Barsh, Marla M. Capozzi, and Jonathan Davidson, "Leadership and Innovation," *The McKinsey Quarterly* 1 (2008): 37–47.

2 Boston Consulting Group, *Innovation 2010: A Return to Prominence—and the Emergence of a New World Order*, Boston, MA, April 2010.

3 My thinking about growth leaders has greatly benefited from a 15-year association with the Mack Institute for Technological Innovation at the Wharton School of the University of Pennsylvania. This research center is the hub of a learning network, supported by industry partners who share a deep interest in profiting from innovation and learning from best practices. For more information about this center, go to whartonmackcenter.com.

4 Peter F. Drucker, *Innovation and Entrepreneurship* (New York: Harper and Row, 1985).

5 Geoff Colvin, "Xerox, Inventor-in-Chief," *Fortune*, July 9, 2007, p. 65.

6 These features have also been identified by other students of innovation, such as: Vijay Govindarajan and Chris Trimble, *Ten Rules for Strategic Innovators: From Idea to Execution*, Boston MA, 2005; Scott D. Anthony, Mark W. Johnson, Joseph V. Sinfield, and Elizabeth J. Altman, *The Innovator's Guide to Growth: Putting Disruptive Innovation to Work* (Boston, MA: Harvard Business School Press, 2008); Michael L. Tushman and Charles A. O'Reilly, *Winning Through Innovation: A Practical Guide to Leading Organizational Change and Renewal* (Boston, MA: Harvard Business School Press, 1997); and Clayton M. Christensen and Michael Raynor, *The Innovator's Solution: Creating and Sustaining Successful Growth* (Boston, MA: Harvard Business School Press, 2003).

7 This expansive view of innovation is consistent with the definition adopted by the Advisory Committee on Measuring Innovation in the 21st Century Economy: "Innovation is the design, invention, development and/or implementation of new or altered products, services, systems or business models for the purpose of creating new value for customers and financial returns for the firm."

8 Scott Sanderude, "Growth from Harvesting the Sky: The $200 Million Challenge," presentation to Marketing Science Institute, Trustees Meeting, Boston, MA, April 15, 2005.

9 Michael Treacy and Jim Sims, "Take Command of Your Growth," *Harvard Business Review* (April 2004): 127–33.

10 W. Chan Kim and Renée Mauborgne, *Blue Ocean Strategy* (Boston, MA: Harvard Business School Press, 2005).

11 Robert G. Cooper, "Your NPD Portfolio May Be Harmful to Your Business Health," *PDMA Visions*, April 2005.

12 George S. Day, "Is It Real? Can We Win? Is It Worth Doing?" *Harvard Business Review* (December 2007), describes how to position growth initiatives on the innovation risk matrix. See also Appendix A.

13 David Robertson, with Bill Breen, *Brick by Brick: How LEGO Reinvented Its Innovation System and Conquered the Toy Industry* (New York: Crown Business, 2013).

14 Daniel Lyons, "The Customer Is Always Right," *Newsweek*, January 4, 2010, pp. 85–86.

15 Edward D. Hess, *The Road to Organic Growth: How Great Companies Consistently Grow Market Share* (New York: McGraw-Hill, 2007).

16 Inder Sidhu, senior vice president, Strategy and Planning, Worldwide Operations, CISCO Systems, speaking to the Mack Center for Technological Innovation Conference on Organizing for Innovation in the "New Normal": Profiting from Uncertainty, November 9, 2012.

17 See Larry Huston and Nabil Sakkab, "Connect and Develop: Inside Proctor & Gamble's New Model for Innovation, *Harvard Business Review* (March 2006): 58–66; and Henry Chesbrough, *Open Business Models: How to Thrive in the New Innovation Landscape* (Boston, MA: Harvard Business School Press, 2006).

18 Constantinos Markides and Paul Geroski, *Fast Second: How Smart Companies Bypass Radical Innovation to Enter and Dominate New Markets* (New York: Jossey-Bass, 2004).

19 See chapter 1 of Anthony, Johnson, Sinfield, and Altman, *The Innovator's Guide to Growth*.

20 Bansi Nagji and Geoff Tuff, "Managing your Innovation Portfolio," *Harvard Business Review* (May 2012): 67–74.

21 "At P&G, the Innovation Well Runs Dry," *BusinessWeek*, September 10–16, 2012, pp. 28–30.

22 For other ways of specifying growth pathways see Mohanbir Sawhney, Robert C. Wolcott, and Inigo Arroniz, "The 12 Different Ways for Companies to Innovate," *MIT Sloan Management Review*, Spring 2006, 75–81, and Geoffrey A. Moore, *Dealing with Darwin*, New York: Portfolio, 2005. Other valuable sources were Clayton Christensen and Michael Raynor, *The Innovator's Solution*, and Rita Gunther McGrath and Ian C. MacMillan, *Market Busters: 40 Strategic Moves That Drive Exceptional Business Growth* (Boston: Harvard Business School Press, 2005).

23 Raphael Amit and Christoph Zott, "Creating Value through Business Model Innovation," *Sloan Management Review* (Spring 2012): 41–49.

24 G. Pohle and M. Chapman, "IBM's Global CEO Report: Business Model Innovation Matters," *Strategy & Leadership* (2006): 34. They found that profit outperformers allocated 38% of their innovation resources to business model innovations, versus 24% by underperformers.

25 For a sampling of this diverse array of methods, see Jim Brown, *Change by Design* (New York: HarperCollins, 2009); Eric Von Hippel, *Democratizing Innovation* (Cambridge MA: MIT Press, 2006); and Gerald Zaltman, *How Customers Think: Essential Insights into the Mind of the Market* (Boston: Harvard Business School Press, 2003).

26 Useful tools for overcoming barriers to nonconsumption are described in Anthony, Johnson, Sinfield, and Altman, *The Innovator's Guide to Growth*, chap. 4.

27 Vijay Govindarajan and Chris Trimble, *Reverse Innovation: Create Far from Home, Win Everywhere* (Boston, MA: Harvard Business School Press, 2012).

28 Kim and Mauborgne, *Blue Ocean Strategy*.

29 Scott Cendrowski, "Nike's New Marketing Mojo," *Fortune*, February 27, 2012, pp. 81–88.

30 I've adopted this phrase from Ranjay Gulati, *Reorganizing for Resilience: Putting Customers at the Center of Your Business* (Boston MA: Harvard Business Press, 2009).

31 For a discussion of how business models in the media industry have been disrupted and the variety of innovative attempts to capture value, see Saul Berman, *Not for Free: Revenue Strategies for a New World* (Boston MA: Harvard Business Press, 2011).

32 Gregory Unruh, *Earth, Inc.: Using Nature's Rules to Build Sustainable Profits* (Boston MA: Harvard Business Press, 2010).

33 Sources include www.curves.com and www.blueoceanstrategy.com/abo/curves/html.

34 Henry Mintzberg, Bruce Ahlstrand, and Joseph Lampel, *Strategy Safari* (New York: Free Press, 1998).

35 This section draws extensively on the work of my colleagues Christian Terwiesch and Karl T. Ulrich, *Innovation Tournaments: Creating and Selecting Exceptional Opportunities* (Boston: Harvard Business Press, 2009). See also Markus Reitzig, "Is Your Company Choosing the Best Innovation Ideas?" *MIT Sloan Management Review* (Summer 2011): 47–52.

36 Alex Kandybin and Vessela Genova, "Big Pharma's Uncertain Future," *Strategy & Business* 66 (2011) 54–63.

37 Terwiesch and Ulrich, *Innovation Tournaments*.

38 This section is adapted from my article, "Is It Real? Can We Win? Is It Worth Doing?" *Harvard Business Review* (December 2007): 3–13.

39 Christopher Bartlett and Afroze Mohammed, "3M Optical Systems: Managing Corporate Entrepreneurship," Harvard Business School Publishing Case 9-395-017 (1994).

40 This section draws extensively on the work of Rita Gunther McGrath and Ian C. MacMillian, *Discovery-Driven Growth: A Breakthrough Process to Reduce Risk and Seize Opportunity* (Boston MA: Harvard Business Press, 2009). My intention here is to highlight the role of DDP and encourage readers to go to this source for hands-on guidance on how to apply it to their project.

41 Terwiesch and Ulrich, *Innovation Tournaments*.

42 This section benefited from the work of McGrath and MacMillan (who offer greater depth on the application of real-options thinking within a portfolio context), and also draws on William F. Hamilton, "Managing Real Options, " in George S. Day and Paul J. H. Schoemaker (with Robert Gunther), *Wharton on Managing Emerging Technologies* (New York: John Wiley and Sons, 2000), pp. 271–88.

43 A good summary of the various studies supporting Figure 3-4 is found in Robert G. Cooper, *Winning at New Products Accelerating the Process from Idea to Launch*, 2nd ed. (Reading, MA: Addison-Wesley, 1993), especially p. 9.

44 In 2012, 3M was selected by BCG as one of the most adaptive companies (where ability to adapt is closely connected to innovation performance). See BCG report by Martin Reeves, Claire Love, and Nishant Mathur, "The Most Adaptive Companies 2012: Winning in an Age of Turbulence," June 2012.

45 I previously used the culture, capabilities, and configuration structure to diagnose market-driven organizations. (There is a great deal of commonality between a market orientation and innovation prowess.) See George S. Day, *The Market-Driven Organization: Understanding, Attracting, and Keeping Valuable Customers* (New York: Free Press, 1999).

46 A. G. Lafley and Ram Charan, *The Game Changer: How You Can Drive Revenue and Profit Growth with Innovation* (New York: Crown Business, 2008).

47 Barry Jaruzelski, John Loehr, and Richard Holman, "The Global Innovation 1000: Why Culture Is Key," Booz & Company (October 25, 2011). (Importance scores were derived from the proportion making the alternate number one of the top 5.)

48 Ahmet H. Kirca, Satish Jayachandran, and William O. Bearden, "Market Orientation: A Meta-Analytic Review and Assessment of Its Antecedents and Impact on Performance, *Journal of Marketing* 69 (2005): 24–41.

49 Gerard J. Tellis, *Relentless Innovation: How to Create a Culture for Market Dominance* (forthcoming 2013).

50 Quoted in Jeffrey H. Dyer, Clayton M. Christensen, and Hal B. Gregersen, *The Innovator's DNA* (Boston, MA: Harvard Business Press, 2011).

51 This section utilizes my work on market learning, and especially Day, *The Market-Driven Organization.*

52 Larry Huston and Nabil Sakkab "Connect and Develop: Inside Procter & Gamble's New Model for Innovation" *Harvard Business Review* (March 2006): 1-B.

53 This section draws on Ron Adner, *The Wide Lens: A New Strategy for Innovation* (New York: Penguin, 2012).

54 Prashant Kale, Harbir Singh, and John Bell, "Relating Well: Building Capabilities for Sustaining Alliance Networks," in Paul R. Kleindorfer and Yoram (Jerry) Wind, eds., *The Network Challenge* (New York: Wharton School Publishing, 2009).

55 For a thorough explication of the stage-gate process, see Robert G. Cooper, *Winning at New Products Accelerating the Process from Idea to Launch*, 2nd ed. (Reading MA: Addison-Wesley, 1993).

56 George Beyer, *Innovation Excellence 2005: How Companies Use Innovation to Improve Profitability and Growth* (Boston: Arthur D. Little, 2005), www.adlittle.com.

57 Robert G. Cooper, "Formula for Success" *Marketing Management*, March/April 2006, pp. 18–24.

58 David Robertson, with Bill Breen, *Brick by Brick: How LEGO Innovation Systems Reinvented Its Innovation System and Conquered the Toy Industry* (New York: Crown Business, 2013).

59 For another perspective on innovation challenges, and possible structural remedies, see Julian Birkinshaw and Morten T. Hansen, "Innovation Value Chain," *Harvard Business Review* B5 (June 2007): 121–30.

60 Robert J. Wolcott and Michael Lippitz, *Grow from Within: Mastering Corporate Entrepreneurship and Innovation* (New York: McGraw-Hill, 2010). The Cargill de-icing chemical example was drawn from their study.

61 These data on innovation metrics came from collaboration between the Mack Center for Technological Innovation at the Wharton School and McKinsey & Co.: The sample was drawn from the McKinsey global database, with 55 percent of the respondents from the C-Suite. This was truly a global study, with 34 percent of respondents from North America, 27 percent from Europe, and 28 percent from Asia.

Index

About the Author

George S. Day is the Geoffrey T. Boisi professor, professor of marketing, and codirector of the Mack Center for Technological Innovation at the Wharton School of the University of Pennsylvania. He was previously the executive director of the Marketing Science Institute. He has been a consultant to numerous corporations, such as General Electric, IBM, Metropolitan Life, Unilever, E.I. du Pont de Nemours, W.L. Gore & Associates, Coca-Cola, Boeing, LG Corp., Best Buy, and Medtronic. He is the past chairman of the American Marketing Association. His primary areas of activity are marketing, the management of emerging technologies, organic growth and innovation, and competitive strategies in global markets.

Day has authored 17 books in the areas of marketing and strategic management. His most recent books are *Strategy from the Outside In: Profiting from Customer Value* (with Christine Moorman) and *Peripheral Vision: Detecting the Weak Signals That Will Make or Break Your Company* (with Paul Schoemaker). He has also been published in the *Harvard Business Review, California Management Review, Strategic Management Journal, Planning Review, Journal of Consumer Research, Journal of Marketing Research, Sloan Management Review,* and *Strategy & Leadership.*

He has won 10 "best article" awards; two of these articles were among the top 25 most influential articles in marketing science in the past 25 years. He was honored with the Charles Coolidge Parlin Marketing Research Award in 1994, the Paul D. Converse Award in 1996, the Sheth Foundation/Journal of Marketing Award in 2003, and the Vijay Mahajan Award in 2001 for career contributions to strategy. In 2003 he received the AMA/Irwin/McGraw-Hill Distinguished Marketing Educator Award.

About the Wharton Executive Essentials Series

The *Wharton Executive Essentials* series from Wharton School Press brings the Wharton School's globally renowned faculty directly to you wherever you are. Inspired by Wharton's Executive Education program, each book is authored by a well-known expert and filled with real-life business examples and actionable advice. Available both as an e-book that is immediately downloadable to any e-reader and as a paperback edition sold through online retailers, each book offers a quick-reading, penetrating, and comprehensive summary of the knowledge that leaders need to excel in today's competitive business environment and capture tomorrow's opportunities.

About Wharton School Press

Wharton School Press, the book publishing arm of The Wharton School of the University of Pennsylvania, was established to inspire bold, insightful thinking within the global business community.

Wharton School Press publishes a select list of award-winning, bestselling, and thought-leading books that offer trusted business knowledge to help leaders at all levels meet the challenges of today and the opportunities of tomorrow. Led by a spirit of innovation and experimentation, Wharton School Press leverages groundbreaking digital technologies and has pioneered a fast-reading business book format that fits readers' busy lives, allowing them to swiftly emerge with the tools and information needed to make an impact. Wharton School Press books offer guidance and inspiration on a variety of topics, including leadership, management, strategy, innovation, entrepreneurship, finance, marketing, social impact, public policy, and more.

Wharton School Press also operates an online bookstore featuring a curated selection of influential books by Wharton School faculty and Press authors published by a wide range of leading publishers.

To find books that will inspire and empower you to increase your impact and expand your personal and professional horizons, visit *wsp.wharton.upenn.edu.*

About The Wharton School

Founded in 1881 as the world's first collegiate business school, the Wharton School of the University of Pennsylvania is shaping the future of business by incubating ideas, driving insights, and creating leaders who change the world. With a faculty of more than 235 renowned professors, Wharton has 5,000 undergraduate, MBA, Executive MBA, and doctoral students. Each year 18,000 professionals from around the world advance their careers through Wharton Executive Education's individual, company-customized, and online programs. More than 99,000 Wharton alumni form a powerful global network of leaders who transform business every day.

For more information, *visit www.wharton.upenn.edu.*

WHARTON ON STRATEGY

\\

KNOWLEDGE FOR ACTION

///

Every good business plan has a strategic plan behind it. But how to implement that strategy is not always a straightforward path. For decades, business executives from around the globe have come to Wharton to gain the strategic knowledge they need to put business plans into action and make an immediate impact on their companies.

At Wharton, our Strategy & Management Programs for executives are for leaders seeking new insights on how to gain competitive advantage for their organizations.

Professor George Day is the Faculty Director of **Innovation for Growth: Strategies and Best Practices**.

WHARTON STRATEGY & MANAGEMENT PROGRAMS:

- **Advancing Business Acumen**
- **Global Strategic Leadership**
- **Making Strategy Work: Leading Effective Execution**
- **Mergers and Acquisitions**
- **Strategic Alliances: Creating Growth Opportunities**
- **Strategic Thinking and Management for Competitive Advantage**

Learn more about our Strategy programs: **www.execed.wharton.upenn.edu**
Contact us at **execed@wharton.upenn.edu** or **+1.215.898.1776** *(worldwide)*.

Printed in the USA
CPSIA information can be obtained
at www.ICGtesting.com
JSHW022146211123
52500JS00003B/27

9 781613 630280